Music in Greek and Roman Culture

DATE DUE

5/14/D4	

E DUE

DEMCO, INC. 38-2931

Ancient Society and History

Music in Greek

Translated by
Rosaria V. Munson

GIOVANNI COMOTTI

and Roman
Culture

The Johns Hopkins University Press
Baltimore and London

The original edition of this book was brought to publication with the generous assistance of the David M. Robinson Fund.

First published as *La musica nella cultura greca e romana*
Copyright © 1979 E.D.T. Edizioni di Torino

Johns Hopkins Paperbacks edition, 1991

The Johns Hopkins University Press, 701 West 40th Street,
Baltimore, Maryland 21211
The Johns Hopkins Press Ltd., London

The paper used in this publication meets the minimum requirements of American National Standard for Information Sciences—Permanence of Paper for Printed Library Materials, ANSI Z39.48-1984.

Library of Congress Cataloging-in-Publication Data

Comotti, Giovanni, 1931–
    Music in Greek and Roman culture.

    Bibliography: p.
    Includes index.
    Translation of: La musica nella cultura greca e romana.
    1. Music, Greek and Roman—History and criticism.
I. Title.
ML169.C6513   1989   780'.938   88-45413
ISBN 0-8018-3364-7 (alk. paper)
ISBN 0-8018-4231-X (pbk.)

Contents

Contents

Abbreviations

Bolisani	E. Bolisani, *Varrone menippeo* (Padua, 1936)
CIG	*Corpus Inscriptionum Graecarum*, vol. 2, ed. A. Boeckh (Berlin, 1843)
Da Rios	*Aristoxeni elementa harmonica*, ed. Rosetta da Rios (Rome, 1954)
Dick	*Martianus Capella*, ed. Adolfus Dick and Jean Préaux (Stuttgart, 1969)
Diehl	*Anthologia lyrica Graeca*, 3d ed., ed. Ernestus Diehl (Leipzig, 1949–52)
Diels-Kranz	*Die Fragmente der Vorsokratiker*, 11th ed., by H. Diels and W. Kranz (Zurich and Berlin, 1964)
Drachmann	*Scholia vetera in Pindari carmina*, vol. 1, ed. A. B. Drachmann (Leipzig, 1903)
Düring	*Die Harmonielehre des Klaudios Ptolemaios*, ed. Ingemar Düring (Göteborg, 1930)

Friedlein *Severini Boetii de institutione arithmetica libri duo, de institutione musica quinque,* ed. G. Friedlein (Leipzig, 1867)

Gardthausen *Ammiani Marcellini rerum gestarum libri qui supersunt,* ed. V. Gardthausen (Leipzig, 1874–75; repr. Stuttgart, 1967)

Gentili *Anacreon,* ed. Bruno Gentili (Rome, 1958)

Hiller *Theonis Smyrnaei Expositio rerum mathematicarum ad legendum Platonem utilium,* ed. E. Hiller (Leipzig, 1878)

Hohl *Scriptores Historiae Augustae,* ed. E. Hohl, Ch. Samberger, and W. Seyfarth (Leipzig, 1965)

Jahn *Censorini de die natali liber,* ed. O. Jahn (Berlin, 1845; repr. Hildesheim, 1965)

Jan *Musici scriptores Graeci: Aristoteles, Euclides, Nicomachus, Bacchius, Gaudentius, Alypius et melodiarum veterum quidquid exstat,* ed. Carl von Jan (Leipzig, 1895; repr. Hildesheim, 1962)

Kemke *Philodemi de musica librorum quae exstant,* ed. J. Kemke (Leipzig, 1884)

Kock *Comicorum Atticorum fragmenta,* 3 vols., ed. Theodorus Kock (Leipzig, 1880–88; repr. Utrecht, 1976)

Lasserre *Plutarque, "De la musique,"* ed., trans., and intr. François Lasserre (Lausanne, 1954)

LP *Poetarum Lesbiorum fragmenta,* ed. E. Lobel and D. L. Page (Oxford, 1955)

Marchesi *Arnobii adversus nationes libri VII,* ed. C. Marchesi (Turin, 1934)

Migne | *Patrologiae cursus completus,* ed. J.-P. Migne, vol. 4 [Ps. Cyprianus] (Paris, 1891); vol. 27 [Hieronymus] (Paris, 1890)

Mynors | *Cassiodori senatoris institutiones,* ed. R. A. B. Mynors (Oxford, 1937, 1963)

Najock | *Anonyma de musica scripta Bellermanniana,* ed. D. Najock (Leipzig, 1975)

Pighi | *Aristoxeni Rhythmica,* ed. and trans. G. B. Pighi (Bologna, 1959)

PMG | *Poetae melici Graeci,* ed. D. L. Page (Oxford, 1962, 1975)

Ribbeck | *Tragicorum Romanorum fragmenta,* 3d ed., O. Ribbeck (Leipzig, 1897)

Sandbach | *Menandri reliquiae selectae,* ed. F. H. Sandbach (Oxford, 1972)

SLG | *Supplementum lyricis Graecis,* ed. D. L. Page (Oxford, 1974)

Snell-Maehler | *Bacchylidis carmina cum fragmentis,* after Bruno Snell, ed. H. Maehler (Leipzig, 1970)

——— | *Pindari carmina cum fragmentis,* vol. 1 [Epinicia], vol. 2 [fragmenta, indices], after Bruno Snell, ed. H. Maehler (Leipzig, 1971–75)

Suda | *Suidae Lexicon,* ed. A. Adler (Leipzig, 1928–38)

Tarditi | *Archilochus,* fragmenta edidit, veterum testimonia collegit. Jo. Tarditi (Rome, 1968)

Wehrli | *Die Schule des Aristoteles,* vol. 2, *Aristoxenos,* 2d ed., text and comm. F. Wehrli (Basel and Stuttgart, 1967)

Willis   *Macrobii Saturnalia, In Somnium Scipionis commentarios*, 2d ed., ed. I. Willis (Leipzig, 1970)

Winnington-Ingram *Aristidis Quintiliani de musica libri tres*, ed. R. P. Winnington-Ingram (Leipzig, 1963)

One

Introduction

Musical Texts and Theoretical Treatises

Anyone who undertakes to write the history of ancient music, Greek and Roman, faces problems very different from those which confront scholars dealing with music of other periods: one is forced to account for the lines of musical development and the most significant moments in musical history, knowing little or nothing about the actual compositions themselves that were produced and performed at the time. Not one note remains from anything that was composed before the third century B.C., and the very few extant Hellenistic and Roman musical texts are so fragmentary and deplorably preserved as to provide little precise information.[1]

Until the middle of the nineteenth century, our knowledge was limited to the hymns traditionally attributed to Mesomedes, a Greek musician from the age of Hadrian (second century A.D.), published by V. Galilei in 1581, and the six instrumental pieces that were inserted as examples in a series of anonymous theoretical writings from late antiquity collected by Bellermann in 1841 under the title *Anonyma de musica scripta Bellermanniana*. Other compositions believed to date from antiquity have been recognized as being by Byzantine or Renaissance scholars of Greek notation: the most famous of these is the fragment of Pindar's *Pythian* 1 (lines 1–8), which Athanasius Kircher published in 1650 in his *Musurgia universalis*. Father Kircher claimed to have discovered it in a manuscript in the library of the San Salvatore convent in Messina, though the manuscript was irretrievably lost after publication in a fire that destroyed the library.

Since 1850 our patrimony of ancient musical texts has been relatively enriched by the discovery of three inscriptions—two Delphic Hymns, the first, anonymous, of 138 B.C., and the second, by Limenius, of 128 B.C.; and the epitaph of Seikilos, of the first century—and of about fifteen short papyrus fragments: the oldest of these, *PLeid.* inv. 510 contains a few lines of Euripides' *Iphigenia in Aulis* and dates from the third century B.C. Performed end to end these compositions would not run as long as a Bach sonata for solo violin; moreover, they are in every case fragmentary, and their interpretation and transcription is often beset with problems.

Scanty also are the cultural indications we can derive from the works of Greek and Roman musical theoreticians, who were concerned almost exclusively with the acoustical and mathematical properties of music. Their theoretical works, moreover, though they constitute a fairly sizeable corpus in terms of the number and the size of the treatises, belong entirely to the Hellenistic and Roman periods. The most ancient of them—the nineteenth book of the pseudo-Aristotelian *Problems* and the *Harmonic Elements* of Aristoxenus, a disciple of Aristotle—date from the third century B.C.

Greek and Roman theoreticians were particularly interested in the doctrine of intervals. They calculated interval size on the basis of numerical relations and analyzed the various ways in which intervals can fall within the tetrachords (basic musical figures, formed by the succession of four notes, which in Greek music serve the same function as the octave scales do for us). They studied larger structures, too, formed by two or more tetrachords. In the *De musica* of Aristides Quintilianus, the *Isagoge* of Baccheius Geron, and the *Isagoge* of Alypius (fifth century), we see employed

2

the musical notation used by the Greeks. But nowhere do we find either reference to any specific musical composition or a detailed account of the technique of composition or performance. It is evident that the authors of these treatises were little concerned with music as it was performed, and only wished to define the theoretical underpinnings of music in the abstract. The motives behind such attitudes can be explained by the traditions of ancient thought. But in any case a lengthy consideration of their works would not contribute appreciably to our knowledge of the history of Greek and Roman musical culture.

Music in Ancient Society

But while musical texts and direct testimony about the technical aspects of composition are too scanty for an extended discussion of ancient musical forms, the literary tradition as a whole provides ample documentation about the occurrence of musical phenomena in ancient culture as to allow a broader and more detailed analysis of its character and sociological aspects.

The Greek term from which our word *music* derived—*mousike* (sc. *techne*), "the art of the Muses"—used to designate, as late as the fifth century B.C., not only the art of making sounds but also poetry and dance. These were the principal means of cultural transmission. Up to the fourth century B.C. Greek culture was primarily oral and was manifested and diffused through public performances, at which speech no less than melody and gesture had decisive functions. The composer of songs for festivals, the poet who sang at banquets, the author of dramatic works, all conveyers of a message, relied for the success of their efforts on the resources of figurative and metaphorical language as well as the harmony of meters and melodies. Thus it is not surprising that in the fifth and fourth centuries B.C. the phrase *mousikos aner* would be used to indicate an educated man, able to comprehend poetic language in its entirety. The unity of poetry, melody, and gesture in archaic and classical culture made the rhythmic-melodic expression contingent on the demands of the verbal text. The simultaneous presence of music, dance, and word in almost all forms of

Figure 1. Bronze statuette of a singing phorminx player. About 700 B.C., roughly contemporary with Homer. Heraklion, Archaeological Museum.

communication suggests also the existence of a widespread musical culture among the Greek peoples from the remotest time. The figurative arts bear witness to intense musical activity as early as the second millennium B.C.: players of stringed and wind instruments are represented in statuettes of the nineteenth through the eighteenth centuries B.C. found in Keros and Thera, and cithara and aulos players appear in Cretan frescoes. In a processional scene from a sarcophagus of the sixteenth century B.C., now in the Heraklion Museum, a procession of women bearing offerings is accompanied by a seven-string lyre. Dance scenes with musical accompaniment are frequently portrayed in vase paintings beginning from the eighth century B.C.[2]

Literary evidence, however, is even more valuable for assessing the role played by music in Greek society as far back as the Mycenaean age. In the *Iliad*, the Achaeans send envoys to the sanctuary of Apollo at Chrysa, on the coast of Asia Minor near modern Edremit, in an attempt to put an end to the plague which had stricken their army outside the walls of Troy. After returning the daughter of the priest Chryses and performing an expiatory sacrifice, they appease the god's wrath by intoning the paean in unison (*Il.* 1.472 ff.). In the *Iliad* (9.185 ff.), Achilles sings and accompanies himself on the phorminx, the stringed instrument of the *aoidoi* (bards), to relieve the pain in his heart. In the scenes of country and city life represented by Hephaestus on the shield of · Achilles, musicians and singers accompany the marriage ceremonies, the workers in the field, and the dances of the young people (*Il.* 18.490 ff.). The *Odyssey* gives considerable scope to the characters of the citharodes Phemius of Ithaca and Demodocus of Corcyra. They appear as true craftsmen of song. Their presence is indispensable if banquets are to be worthy of noble guests, and they provide accompaniment to athletic dances during the festival of the Phaeacians. These singers have a vast and well-tested repertoire of songs which their habitual audience knows and appreciates (*Od.* 1.377 ff.; 8.487 ff.). They are honored as repositories of inspiration, the sacred gift of the Muses, and as artists capable of expounding suitably and effectively the themes which the goddesses themselves suggest.[3]

While numerous and interesting allusions to musical activity can be found in the Homeric poems, literary evidence from later times reveals a far more intense and complex musical life. All Greek lyrical texts, both archaic and classical, were composed to be sung accompanied by an instrument in front of an audience. In dramatic performances of the classical period, choral and solo singing were at least as important as dialogue and dramatic actions. Music played a role in every moment of Greek communal life—in religious ceremonies, competitions, symposia, festivals, even in political contentions, as the songs of Alcaeus and Timocreon of Rhodes demonstrate.

The singing of Orpheus appeases beasts and persuades the gods of Hades to return Eurydice to the light; Amphion and Zethus build the walls of Thebes, moving stones by the sound of their lyre—to cite only two examples out of many. Both the mythological and the literary evidence, starting right from Homer himself, reveal the ascendant role that song and the sound of instruments played in initiatory, purificatory, apotropaic, medical, and other kinds of rituals. We shall consider the psychagogic power the Greeks attributed to music when we examine Pythagorean theories and the *ethos* of the *harmoniai* in the doctrine of Damon. The function of song and musical instruments in magical practices is amply documented by ethnomusicological research. Studies of music in so-called primitive societies reveal correspondences and similarities with the musical manifestations of archaic Greece and can in many cases provide a stimulating contribution to our understanding.

General conclusions regarding the importance of music in the communal and cultural life of Greece preserve their validity when transferred to the Roman world. As far as musical phenomena are concerned, Rome in the earliest phase appears closely analogous to archaic Greece. Within Rome's oral culture, all the poetic forms we know about—religious poetry, convivial songs, dramatic texts, triumphal songs, funerary lamentations—were designed to be sung with instrumental accompaniment. One should not forget that since the Mycenaean age, as recent archaeological discoveries have shown, Rome and Latium had frequent relations with the Greek world both through direct commerce and the contact with southern Italy and through the mediation of the Etruscans. Because of the increasingly close ties between Roman and Greek civilizations, after the start of the third century B.C. there no longer appeared to be substantial differences between the forms of musical expression in the two cultures.

Composition, Diffusion, and Transmission of Musical Texts

Why is it that nothing has come down to us of so vast a musical legacy, even though a fair number of Greek and Latin literary works, constituting the textual support of song, have been preserved? In order to answer this question, we must confront the problem of the transmission of musical texts, a problem that necessarily involves a look at the technique of composition and the manner of diffusion.[4]

Because of the strict correlation between poetry, music, and dance, the results of recent studies on the composition and especially on the diffusion of literary texts illuminate rhythmical and musical components as well. One must first of all emphasize that each performance adhered strictly to the *hic et nunc:* the occasion of the song conditioned its performance at the textual, rhythmical, and melodic levels. Each composition could subsequently be repeated at different times, as happened especially in the case of sympotic songs, but its elements—words, rhythm, and music— were each time adjusted to the requirements of the moment, even though they always preserved a certain conformity of style, metrical structure, and modulation which guaranteed the continuity of the song's character in spite of variations and improvisations. The diffusion and transmission of texts took place through listening and memorization. Even when poets no longer improvised, but rather wrote down their compositions, these continued to be known to the audience through oral performance.

As far as music in particular is concerned, we know that it faithfully maintained the traditional forms of composition down to the end of the fifth century B.C. This adherence must necessarily have meant the continuous repetition of structural and melodic schemes which constituted the characteristic elements of the particular genres of song. Plato (*Laws* 3.700a ff.) recalls that in the past the various musical genres were clearly distinct, and each had its specific character: the prayer to the gods, the hymn, would not be confused with the dirge, the paean, the dithyramb, or the nomos. Composers were not at liberty to attribute to these forms of song a different purpose than the one tradition prescribed. For Plato, to violate this law would herald the dissolution of the social and political order as well:

> Those who keep watch over our commonwealth must take the greatest care not to overlook the least infraction of the rule against any innovation upon the established system of education either of the body or of the mind. When the poet says that men care most for "the newest air that hovers over the singer's lips," they will be afraid lest he be taken not merely to mean new songs, but to be commending a new style of music. Such innovation is not to be commended, nor should the poet be so understood. The introduction of novel fashions in music is a thing to beware of as endangering the whole fabric of society, whose most important conventions are unsettled by any revolution in that quarter. So Damon declares, and I believe him. (*Rep.* 4.424b–c; trans. Cornford)

Greek musical composition down to the fourth century B.C. maintained this dual character of improvisation-variation according to the requirements of the moment and, at the same time, of repetitiveness in deference to tradition. The composer suited his song to the occasion without modifying the essential, inviolable elements of the genre.[5]

On the strength of these considerations, there is reason to believe that down to the fourth century B.C. Greeks felt no need to write music. Melody was substantially repetitive, since within the range of possible variations, it conformed to traditional melodic patterns. The teaching of song and of instrumental music was aural. This fact is attested in vase paintings, such as the representation of master and pupil on the *skyphos* by Pistoxenus,[6] and is suggested by Plato (*Laws* 7.812d).

Another argument *ex silentio* tends to confirm the hypothesis that in the archaic and classical ages music was never written down: the manuscript tradition of the Greek poets, which in great

Figure 2. Skyphos by Pistoxenus showing Linus and Iphicles at a music lesson. About 470 B.C. Schwerin, Staatliche Museum.

part goes back to editions prepared by Alexandrian grammarians, has preserved no text with musical notation. If in Hellenistic times editors had been in a position to transcribe melodic lines along with literary texts, they almost certainly would have done so.

The first piece of evidence suggesting the use of some form of notation appears in Aristoxenus (*Harm.* 1.7, p. 12, 15 Da Rios), who wrote between the end of the fourth century and the beginning of the third century B.C. His references do not concern musical writing as practiced by contemporary composers, but rather its use by theoreticians. Nor do vase paintings, which according to some scholars would prove the existence of texts with musical notes beginning from the early fifth century, provide certain proof. Some vases represent musicians who sing or play an instrument in front of papyrus rolls, but one should not therefore assume that these rolls had musical notes written on them.[7] In the case of the Berlin krater (Berlin 2549F), the painter has traced alphabetic signs on a *volumen* kept open by a youth, and the placing of the signs in sparse array has suggested the hypothesis, maintained by E. Pöhlmann himself, that they represent musical notes.

In the last century scholars assumed that musical notation was

Figure 3. Kylix by Douris showing school scenes: instruction in playing the lyre (upper); lessons in singing (lower). Berlin 2285.

already in use in the seventh through sixth centuries B.C. Westphal first advanced the hypothesis, which became generally accepted, that the musical signs that did not correspond to the letters of the Attic alphabet were taken from a seventh-century Argive alphabet. In fact, as has been recently demonstrated by A. Bataille and J. Chailley, the succession of musical signs such as we know it from Aristides Quintilianus, Baccheius, and Alypius cannot antedate the fourth century B.C. The signs themselves were probably modified from the characters of the Attic alphabet.

Hence there are valid reasons for believing that Greek music was never written down prior to the fourth century and that even later on musical writing was employed solely by professional musicians. Greek literary texts were never published with musical scores, not even after the fourth century, when the diffusion and transmission of poetry took place in written form as well as through performance. The few examples we have of texts with musical notes are most likely promptbooks annotated by singers, instrumentalists, and teachers, designed for circulation within the narrow milieu of a chorus, a theatrical company, or a school.[8] It is significant that the papyri which bear literary texts with musical notations should almost all be of dramatic works. The sole exceptions are two rather late fragments, *PBerol.* 6870, of the second to third centuries (a paean), and *POxy.* 1786, of the third to fourth centuries (a Christian hymn). *PLeid.* inv. 510 (third century B.C.) contains a selection of passages from Euripides' *Iphigenia in Aulis,* and *POsl.* 1413 (first or second century) has two fragments of an unknown tragedy. They seem therefore to represent anthologies of dramatic texts for use by *tragodoi,* virtuoso actors of Hellenistic and Roman times.[9] The three inscriptions with musical notes—the two Delphic hymns and Seikilos's epitaph—are evidence, in the first case, of the pride of a composer and of a chorus who performed successfully at Delphi, and, in the second, of the "melomania" of a musician who chose to have his tombstone inscribed with a brief composition.

That so little has remained of ancient music is accordingly not surprising. Compositions were entrusted only to the memory of the listeners and reelaborated in the course of individual performances. They were lost when, on account of changing tastes, the need was no longer felt to take them up again. Polybius (*Hist.* 4.20–21) mentions that in the second century B.C. the melodies of Timotheus continued to be performed only in some very remote villages of Arcadia—in provincial areas, that is, with respect to the most lively centers of contemporary culture. And yet, only two centuries earlier, the innovations introduced by Timotheus himself had practically revolutionized the entire traditional musical culture. If in the second century the "new music" of dithyramb composers was all but forgotten in Athens, we should not marvel at the fact that memory of musical compositions from archaic and classical times had disappeared as well.

Two

Greek Music

The Origins

Before confronting the problem of the origins of ancient musical forms, one must first state a basic proposition, valid for the archaic period and for subsequent times alike: the Greeks and the Romans did not know harmony, in the modern sense of the term, or polyphony; their music expressed itself through pure melodic line alone. The accompaniment faithfully followed the development of the song, either in unison or at the interval of an octave. Only after the fourth century B.C. do we know of songs accompanied at an interval of a fourth or a fifth.

Music, then, was simple and linear and, at least until the last decades of the fifth century B.C., functioned mainly to characterize the text in relation to its poetic "genre," its purpose, and the occasion of performance.[1] When Pindar, at the beginning of *Olympian* 2, invokes the hymns as "lords of the lyre," he wishes to signify the subordination of music to poetry. Likewise, the rhythm of the musical performance was conditioned by the metrical form of the verse. One should keep in mind that Greek and Latin meter was based on the quantity of the syllables, not on the position of stress or tonic accents, as is the case with modern Western languages. Verse structure was determined by the patterned succession of long and short syllables and involved the alternation of strong and weak beats, which produced the verse rhythm. The two-to-one ratio between the duration of long and short syllables was scrupulously observed in the performance of song until the musical reform of Timotheus (fifth to fourth century B.C.). Afterwards composers would deal freely with the chronic value of the metrical elements, sometimes lengthening the duration of a long syllable up to five beats. A rhythmical theory text preserved in a papyrus from the third century (*POxy*. 9 + 2687) explains the manner of diction of Hellenistic performers who adapted the rhythm of the metrical pattern to the requirements of the music.

Reliable evidence regarding the origin of Greek music is preserved by the author of the dialogue *De musica,* attributed to Plutarch.[2] It is a particularly valuable source because it is based on the works of Pythagorean, Academic, and Peripatetic scholars, such as Glaucus of Rhegium, Heraclides Ponticus, and Aristoxenus, who were well informed about the musical culture of archaic Greece. In the dialogue's first chapters, Lysias, one of the characters, names those to whom the institution of the various poetic-musical genres was attributed: Amphion, son of Zeus, invented citharody (song accompanied by the cithara), Linus the *threnoi* (funeral songs), Anthes the *hymnoi*. Among the citharodes, Pierus composed verses in honor of the Muses; Philammon was the first to instruct a chorus to honor Leto, Apollo, and Artemis; Thamyris sang the Titanomachy, Demodocus the destruction of Ilium (cf. *Od.* 8.487 ff.) and the marriage of Aphrodite and Hephaestus (cf. *Od.* 8.266 ff.), and Phemius the return of the heroes from the Trojan war (cf. *Od.* 1.325 ff.).[3] A special place is reserved by Pseudo-Plutarch for Orpheus, the Thracian singer, mentioned above all for the originality of his compositions ("Orpheus seems never to have imitated anyone," *De mus.* 5).

Besides the citharodes, he names the auletai—players of the aulos, a reed wind instrument common in various forms throughout the eastern Mediterranean—and the aulodes, composers of songs to be accompanied by the aulos. Among the first are listed

Olympus, Hyagnis, Marsyas, and Olympus the Younger, all originally from Phrygia, a fact which indicates the close musical connection from remotest times between Greece and Asia Minor. In
the second group, the author mentions Ardalus of Troezen, Clonas, and Polymnestus, authors of elegies and lyric songs.

Some of these composers supposedly lived and were active
before or during the time in which the Homeric epic poems took
shape. According to Pseudo-Plutarch (*De mus.* 3), they composed
monodic and choral songs, probably in lyric meter. On the
strength of an observation which the author borrows from Heraclides Ponticus, we may surmise that their songs could already
have been structured according to the triadic scheme characteristic
of choral lyric from Stesichorus onward (i.e., strophe, followed by
an antistrophe which repeated the strophe's exact metrical form,
followed in turn by an epode which concluded the triad, serving to
link the subsequent triad): "[Heraclides says] that the poetic texts
of the authors we have just listed [Thamyris, Demodocus, Phe-
mius] were not made up of free rhythms, without regular measure,
but were structurally identical to the texts of Stesichorus and the
other lyric poets who composed epic verses and set them to music"
(*De mus.* 3).

This passage of Pseudo-Plutarch confirms the very plausible
hypothesis that between pre-Homeric sung poetry and the lyric
poetry of the archaic and classical periods there is no break in
continuity.[4] We must instead assume that from this sung poetry,
epic in subject, which began to flourish in Greece during the last
period of the Mycenaean age, two distinct poetic genres emerged:
(1) through a process of metrical normalization, the hexameter
poetry of the rhapsodes, recited rather than sung, such as the great
Homeric epics (the *Iliad* and the *Odyssey*) and the theological and
didactic poetry of Hesiod (the *Theogony* and *Works and Days*); and
(2) all the vast lyric production of subsequent periods.

The development of intense poetic and musical activity after the
end of the Mycenaean age is connected with the profound change
which Greek society underwent just at this time, a change that was
substantially univocal in spite of its diverse pace and manifestations in different parts of Greece. The relationship between town

and country ceased to be one of sheer contrast, as it had been earlier when the king from his fortified citadel subjected the surrounding countryside to his rule. The two became integrated, with the fringes of the newly established *polis,* the city-state, coinciding with the regional borders in a pattern of territorial organization that had no precedent in the ancient world.

This new political structure gave citizens increasing opportunities for participating in the different forms of community life: religious festivals, ceremonies of the *thiasoi* (associations of the initiated in the cults of certain gods), and banquets of the *hetairiai* (for those belonging to one or another political faction). Public festivals included as a rule the performance of choral compositions, according to their purpose. The most ancient were the *paian,* in honor of Apollo, the *linos,* the *hymenaios* (a wedding song), and the *threnos* (a funeral song), all mentioned already in Homer. To these, others were added, such as the *hymnos,* a song in honor of gods or men; the *prosodion,* a processional melody; the *partheneion,* a maidens' song; and the *dithyrambos,* which is Dionysiac in character.[5]

Monodic songs were usually designed for a more restricted audience, such as that of the *thiasoi* and, especially, of the symposia at the end of banquets, when the guests, after the ritual libations to the gods, would give themselves over to the pleasures of wine and love. But symposia also provided the occasion for exchanges of ideas, for political debates, and for programs of action. Music and song not only contributed to making this communal experience more pleasurable but often became the instruments of political and cultural propaganda, as can be seen from the poems of Alcaeus and many archaic elegies.

The nomoi. Music in Sparta

At the beginning, the musical landscape was diverse. Each region had its repertoire of melodies for different occasions, handed down orally from generation to generation. Gradually the most significant and popular melodies were exported from their places of origin through the effort of musicians who "gave them a name"

(Ps.-Plut. *De mus.* 3), so that each might be individually recognizable by all the Greeks. These melodic forms were referred to as *nomoi,* the same term used to signify "the laws"; Pseudo-Plutarch explains the reasons for this analogy between the legal and musical spheres:[6] "in ancient times it was not possible to compose citharodic pieces like those of today, nor to change *harmonia* or rhythm, but for each of the *nomoi* the songs maintained their special characteristics. For this reason they were named thus, *nomoi* [i.e., "laws"], because it was not legitimate to exceed the limits of tuning and character prescribed for each of them" (*De mus.* 6).

The nomes were well-defined melodic structures, each of which was intended for a particular ritual occasion. The title of each referred to its place of origin, as in the case of the Boeotian and Aeolian nomes; or to its formal features, as the Orthios, Trochaic, and Acute nomes (where the terms refer to the rhythmic form or to the tonal range); or to its sacral destination, such as the Pythian nome, or the nomes of Zeus, Athena, and Apollo.

The regularizing of the nomes can be regarded as the first personal intervention of a composer on traditional musical material. Pseudo-Plutarch gives credit for this first of all to Terpander (eighth to seventh century B.C.), a musician from Antissa on the island of Lesbos who moved to Sparta, established a music school there, and gained renown by a victory at the Carneans, the musical competitions in honor of Apollo first held at the time of the Twenty-sixth Olympiad (676–73 B.C.). According to other sources, Terpander is also supposed to have perfected the *lyra* by increasing the number of its strings from four to seven. We know, however, that the heptachord had already been in use for many centuries, so that this information merely suggests the fame Terpander enjoyed as a citharode. Analogous contributions to the normalization of the nomes were made in the same period by other musicians: Clonas for the aulodic, and Olympus the Younger for the auletic nomes.

The original meaning of *nomos* was, as we have seen, "tune, traditional melody": Alcman, a few decades after Terpander, states in a fragment quoted by Athenaeus (*PMG* fr. 40.) that he knows the *nomoi* of all the birds. Later on, however, the term was used to denote a specific citharodic solo song, a well-defined musical genre which would be taken up again by Timotheus between the fifth and the fourth centuries B.C. Pollux (*Onom.* 4.66) provides information about its structure, supposedly defined by Terpander himself: it consisted of seven parts, called *archa* (initial song), *metarcha* (in rhythmic responsion with the *archa*), *katatropa* (transition), *metakatatropa* (in rhythmic responsion with the *katatropa*), *omphalos* ("navel," the central part), *sphragis* ("seal," in which the author talked about himself), and the *epilogos* (the conclusion). Some commentators apply this scheme to all the nomes without distinction and not, as we have said, to a particular type of citharodic and soloistic nome. But Pollux himself (*Onom.* 4.84) attributes a different structure to the auletic Pythian nome, which described in five sections Apollo's fight with the serpent, and Pseudo-Plutarch (*De mus.* 8) mentions a *nomos Trimeres,* aulodic and choral, composed by Sacadas of Argos (seventh to sixth century), which consisted of just three parts, each very different from the other two in its melodic formulation.

A second music school was founded in Sparta by Thaletas of Gortyn a few decades after Terpander's own; to it belonged Xenodamus of Cythera, Xenocritus of Locris, Polymnestus of Colophon, and Sacadas of Argos, to whom Pseudo-Plutarch attributes the institution of such musical festivals as the *Gymnopaidiai* at Sparta, the *Apodeixeis* in Arcadia, and the *Endymatia* at Argos. These musicians devoted themselves especially to composing choral songs, and although they respected traditional melodic forms, they introduced some innovations—for instance, the use of the paeon and the cretic, measures of five times from the rhythmic genre *hemiolion,* which Thaletas supposedly borrowed from Olympus.

In the seventh century, then, Sparta was the most important musical center of Greece.[7] Music and gymnastics formed the basis of education for boys and girls, who, after seven years of age, were schooled in common by the state. Choral song was meant to fulfill a paideutic function with regard to the community as a whole because it reinforced essential values of public morality, such as love for the fatherland and respect for the law. In this cultural environment, musicians from all of Greece made considerable contributions to the repertory of Spartan songs. Here, in addition to the authors already spoken of, I should mention Ardalus of Troezen, Clonas of Tegea, Pythocritus of Argos, and Pericletus of Lesbos.

Alcman, who was perhaps originally from Lydia, lived and was active in Sparta in the second half of the seventh century B.C. He composed *partheneia* for communities of young women who through rites of passage from adolescence to adulthood were initiated to married life.[8] Pseudo-Plutarch mentions that Alcman had cited in his verses the name of Polymnestus, thereby alluding to a derivation of his melodies from the nomes of that ancient aulode. Alcman himself, however, maintains in a fragment (*PMG* fr. 39) that he "invented verses and melodies" and "composed the voice of partridges."[9] Elsewhere (*PMG* fr. 40), he says that he knows the voices of all the birds. These statements bear witness to innovations in the traditional *melos*, innovations which the poet claims to have been the first to introduce, by saying that he has imitated nature rather than previous authorities. In yet another fragment (*PMG* fr. 14) Alcman insists on the novelty of his song, and Himerius (*Or.* 39.12) mentions that he performed Lydian tunes on the Dorian lyre—he introduced, that is, Lydian melodies to the Spartans. Athenaeus (14.636f ff.) cites lines from a poem of Alcman's that mention the *magadis*, an instrument of Lydian origin with twenty strings positioned in such a way as to resound two by two at the interval of an octave. The same Athenaeus (14.624b) records the names of famous Phrygian auletai whom Alcman mentioned in his verses. Strabo (12.8.21), speaking about the Phrygians, cites another Alcman line ("he performed on the aulos the Phrygian *melos kerbesion,*" *PMG* fr. 126), thus confirming the close connection his poetry had to Asiatic musical culture.

The Musical Schools of the Seventh and Sixth Centuries B.C.

Thaletas of Gortyn introduced to Sparta the innovations of Archilochus of Paros, slightly older than himself. Archilochus had used in his compositions iambic rhythms ($\smile - \smile -$, rhythms that were classed as double because of the ratio 1 : 2 between the duration of short and long syllables) and trochaic (– ◡ – ◡, also classed as double, but with the long syllable preceding the short one), as well as asynartetic verses, constituting the juxtaposition of two autonomous rhythmic elements (cola), and the epodic structure, formed by the succession of a longer line and a shorter one. He supposedly introduced in addition the parakataloge, a form of recitative supported by the music of the aulos (comparable to the recitar cantando of eighteenth-century melodrama), with the accompaniment no longer playing in unison, but at an octave interval.[10]

Archilochus's production was not limited to the monodic form. He himself states that he composed dithyrambs: "I know how to intone the beautiful song of lord Dionysus, the dithyramb, when I am lightning-struck by wine in my soul" (fr. 77D = 117 Tarditi). He also composed a hymn to Heracles (fr. 207 Tarditi) which he sang personally at Olympia alternating with the chorus (cf. Schol. Pind. Ol. 9.1a, 1:266 Drachmann). But unfortunately, we have no information on the nature of Archilochean melodies. The geographical position of Paros, near the coast of Asia Minor, leads us to believe that the island's traditional songs had characteristics analogous to those of Ionia, famous in antiquity for the sophistication and elegance of its music.

In the seventh to sixth centuries Lesbos, another island near the Asiatic coast, was the center of intense musical activity and acquired influence and renown far beyond its shores. I have already mentioned Terpander, who moved to Laconia from Antissa. From Lesbos came Pericletus (who, like Terpander, was a victor at the Carnean festival in Sparta), and Arion of Methymna.

The surviving songs of Alcaeus and Sappho, as well as the ancient testimony regarding their poetic activity, reveal close cultural contacts between Lesbos and the nearby kingdom of Lydia. In the sphere of music, Aristoxenus (Ps.-Plut. De mus. 20 = fr. 81 Wehrli) attributes to Sappho the merit of having created the Mixolydian harmonia, meaning that her compositions combined Lesbian tunes with musical forms from Asia Minor. Originally from Lydia were certainly some musical instruments mentioned by the two poets, such as the pektis (Alcaeus fr. 36 LP; Sappho fr. 156 LP), a kind of high-pitched harp, and the *barbitos*, or *baromos*, or *barmos* (Alcaeus fr. 70.4 *LP;* Sappho fr. 176 *LP*), a lyre with very long strings and therefore low in tone. According to Athenaeus (14.635a), Sappho used to accompany her songs with the *magadis*, a Lydian instrument which had been known to Alcman. This evidence points to a continuous interaction between two different musical cultures, an interaction suggested by the presence *ab antiquo* in Greece of auletic melodies of Phrygian origin.

Alcaeus and Sappho lived in Mytilene between the seventh and the sixth centuries B.C., a time of bitter political struggle. The equilibrium among aristocratic factions which had earlier maintained the oligarchic government had broken down, and the various city leaders competed with one another for personal power. Melanchrus and Myrsilus, of the Cleanactid family, prevailed by force of arms (*tyrannoi*). Pittacus, on the other hand, was called on by a consensus of the citizens to solve the institutional problems of the state through a redaction of new laws (*aisymnetes*). In this same period, many other Greek cities saw their oligarchic governments replaced by forms of tyrannical power. Just as happened in Mytilene, Pittachus succeeded in reestablishing peace and harmony, and in most cases elsewhere the rise of *tyrannoi* or *aisymnetai* had positive results, not only because it helped the *poleis* to achieve internal peace but also because it hastened their social and political evolution.

In this climate of civil strife and personal animosities, Alcaeus composed his songs mainly for the benefit of his companions in the political struggle, the members of his faction. The occasion of the song was the banquet, or symposium, of the *hetairoi*. During the symposium the poet, accompanying himself on the *barbitos*, would first invoke the gods in a short hymn and then recall the causes of the struggle, attack his adversaries, and exhort his audience not to give in to the opposition. But for Alcaeus the symposium was both the occasion for paraenesis and political propaganda as well as the moment of pleasure, of wine, and of love, themes which had their place within the repertoire of political songs only as brief interludes in the storms of civil war.

The poetic activity of Sappho, on the other hand, took place exclusively within the *thiasos*. This was the center of a cult sacred to Aphrodite, the Muses, and the Charites, and the seat of a community of girls from the Lesbian and Ionian aristocracy, as a recently discovered papyrus testifies (*SLG* fr. 261a). The *thiasos* represented the principal instrument of the girls' education and of their initiation to married life at the time of their passage from adolescence to adulthood Essential components of this paideutic process were music, dance, and song, strictly connected to the community's rituals and to wedding initiation ceremonies. On the strength of testimony from Himerius (*Or.* 1.4), it is legitimate to assume that a good part of Sappho's wedding songs—epithalamians—were meant to be performed by the girls' chorus during marriage ceremonies.[11] The melodic sequences on which these songs were modulated had evidently a very simple structure that conformed to the metrical figures of the poetic text. An analogous simplicity of musical texture must have characterized the melodies of monodic songs, which Sappho sang to the girls of her community, and which Alcaeus addressed to political partisans.

The colonies of Southern Italy and Sicily, at the outskirts of the Greek world, saw the rise of a musical and poetic school whose most distinguished representative was Stesichorus of Himera, a composer of both monodic and choral songs. His sobriquet Stesichorus (Teisias was his real name) testifies to his activity as instructor of choruses. The prevalence in his work of epic-mythological subjects, and his constant use of the strophic triad (strophe, antistrophe, epode) and of cithara accompaniment, identify him as heir of the oldest pre-Homeric citharodic tradition. Glaucus of Rhegium (Ps.-Plut. *De mus.* 7) connects him to the oldest Phrygian aulete, Olympus, from whose repertoire Stesichorus borrowed the *nomos Harmateios,* the "chariot melody" of Phrygian origin, which probably used to be performed in the ceremonies of the cult of Cybele. According to Glaucus, moreover, Stesichorus derived from Olympus the use of dactylic rhythms classed as even (i.e., in which the syllabic elements have equal duration), typical of the *nomos Orthios,* or "high-pitched" melody, again a tune of Phrygian or

21

Mysian origin. The meters which Stesichorus employed in most of his compositions reveal in fact dactylic or anapaestic melodic structures of the even sort side by side with the so-called dactylo-epitrites, where the metrical feet, or *cola*, such as the *hemiepes*, the enoplion, and the prosodiac of mixed classes (even and double together), are combined with iambs and trochees of epitritic form. The presence in Stesichorus's work of musical elements from different traditions testifies to the spread by the end of the seventh century of the melodic forms of the nomes. While preserving their original features, these had become a part of the common musical heritage of Greece.

The same musical environment to which Stesichorus belonged produced Ibycus of Rhegium, who was active at the court of Polycrates, tyrant of Samos, around 564–61 B.C., if we follow the dating offered by the *Suda*. In the small extant corpus of Ibycus's verses, references to his musical activity are few, and ancient testimony as to his life and poetry similarly provides only slight indications. It is reasonable to suppose that during the time he spent at the court of Polycrates, Ibycus would have added Ionian melodies to his Southern Italian repertory of Dorian tunes. From Neanthes of Cyzicus (Athen. 4.175e) we learn that he sometimes accompanied his songs with the *sambyke*, a polychord instrument of Asiatic origin akin to the *magadis* used by Alcman and Sappho. He must have employed auloi too, if it is true that he composed dithyrambs (*Schol. Eur. Andr.* 631 = *PMG* fr. 299).

Anacreon of Teos was active in Samos in the second part of the sixth century B.C. After the defeat of Polycrates by the Persians (522 B.C.), he was guest of Hipparchus, tyrant of Athens. Anacreon was the author of monodic songs which he performed at the symposia of tyrannic courts. A single, and rather dubious, testimony (fr. 190 Gentili) attributes to him the composition of choral songs for girls (*partheneia*). Teos, on the Ionian coast, had been the city of Pythermus, another lyric poet, the author of drinking songs and singer of Ionian melodies (Athen. 14.625c). It is probable that Anacreon was educated at the same school and that his themes took inspiration from the musical tradition of his land. Moreover, the poet himself mentions in his verses, beside the *lyra* and the auloi, instruments of Asiatic origin, specifically the *pektis*, the *magadis*, and the *barbitos*, which Alcaeus and Sappho had referred to in their compositions and which must have been in common use throughout Ionia. Like Alcaeus and Sappho, Anacreon addresses a narrow, culturally homogeneous audience. Shared lexical elements (especially with Sappho) and the use of analogous metrical structures and instruments, give us reason to suppose that Anacreon was familiar with the compositions of the two Lesbian poets.[12]

The Dithyramb. Lasus and the harmoniai. *Pythagoras.*

In Corinth, at the beginning of the sixth century B.C., Dionysiac cult song underwent a profound transformation in its structure and manner of performance thanks to the work of Arion. Arion lived at a time and in a milieu which were particularly propitious for the dithyrambic genre, inasmuch as the tyrants favored the cult of Dionysus, a divinity honored by all classes of people, as opposed to the primarily aristocratic cults of other gods and heroes.[13]

The nature of Arion's activity is explained by two sources—Herodotus (1.23) and the lexicon *Suda* (s.v.)—which state that he composed and named the dithyramb, and taught it to the chorus. According to the *Suda*, he was also the inventor of the tragic genre and introduced satyrs who spoke in verse. Arion, in other words, gave definition and identity to Dionysiac songs ("gave them their names") in the same way as his fellow citizen Terpander and the seventh-century musicians regularized the nomes. In Arion's dithyramb the satyrical elements of old fertility songs mixed with oriental motifs, especially those of Phrygian origin, which would have already been familiar throughout the Hellenic world as essential components in the tunes accompanying Dionysiac rites. Arion was said in addition to have changed the formation of the dithyrambic chorus from square to circular. This information is given by Proclus (*Chrest.* 43), who traces it back to Aristotle. If my interpretation of the Proclus passage is correct, the choral dancers no longer moved in straight lines according to the scheme of processional dances but, rather, from their position around the altar of the god, performed circular evolutions, first in one direction (strophe), then in the other according to the same rhythmical pattern (antistrophe), and, finally, with movements limited to a restricted space (epode). The triadic form of dance performance, which Stesichorus certainly took from the oldest citharodoi, was supposedly reproduced by Arion himself, who adapted them to the new Dionysiac dance. Here the performance in a circular space surrounded by the audience emphasized the scenic component.

But the dithyramb became the special focus of attention by composers after the middle of the sixth century. In Athens at this time Pisistratus instituted the festival of the City Dionysia, at which dithyrambic, tragic, and comic contests represented the most important events. The competitive climate that prevailed among the participants in the contests must have tended to counteract the ritualistic and repetitive character of dithyrambic song, and began a process of secularization which would become marked with the work of such composers as Melanippides, Cinesias, and Timotheus in the second half of the century. The poetic texts would no longer deal exclusively with Dionysiac myths, but would also deal with episodes in the lives of other gods and heroes. As far as rhythm and melody were concerned, as we shall see, composers now felt little obligation to adhere slavishly to traditional schemes and tunes. At once respecting the integrity of the poetic genre by employing musical elements derived from the repertoire of the oldest dithyrambic songs, they introduced innovations in the melodic pattern.

This different way of interpreting adherence to tradition soon spread to the other genre of choral lyric: the *nomos*—the ritual song, which by its very nature was bound to remain substantially unchanged in its melodic elements—was replaced by compositions supported by a new structural framework called the *harmonia*. The original meaning of this term was "joint, connection, adaptation" (cf. Hom. *Od.* 5.248), and therefore "pact, convention"; in its musical sense, the first meaning was "tuning of an instrument" and, consequently, "disposition of the intervals within a scale." But for the writers of the sixth to fifth century B.C., *harmonia* had a much broader semantic range than "modal scale," which is the meaning the theoreticians of Hellenistic and Roman times attributed to the word.[14] *Harmonia* signified a combination of features which together denoted a certain type of musical discourse: not only a particular disposition of the intervals but also specific pitch, modulation, color, intensity, and timbre, all the elements which distinguish the musical output of a particular geographical and cultural environment. Ancient authors used to qualify the harmoniae by adjectives and adverbs—e.g., *aiolis,* "Aeolian," or *aiolisti,* "in the Aeolic manner"—which made specific reference to the musical traditions of individual regions. It is not by chance that most of the nomes and melodies of which we have spoken earlier originated precisely from those areas of Greece and Asia Minor which gave their names to the Aeolian, Dorian, Lydian, Phrygian, and Ionian harmoniae. Unfortunately, we do not possess the criteria for defining with any accuracy the specific features of each individual harmonia. Plato, however (*Rep.* 3.398e ff.), defines the Syntonolydian and the Mixolydian (two varieties of the Lydian harmonia) as plaintive, the Ionian and the Lydian as "slack" and appropriate to drinking parties, the Dorian as virile and determined, and the Phrygian as suitable for peaceful action and persuasion. Heraclides Ponticus (Athen. 14.624c) indicates in somewhat less general terms some of the elements which mark off the Dorian from the Ionian and Aeolian harmoniae. He compares the virile, austere, strong character of the first with the stately solemnity of the Aeolian mode; with regard to the Ionian harmonia, he notes a nobility not devoid of hardness—characteristics peculiar to the more ancient tunes as opposed to the sweetness and softness of the modern ones.

The term *harmonia,* in the sense I have just illustrated, occurs for the first time in a fragment of Lasus of Hermione, a citharode from the Peloponnese who around 520 B.C. moved to Athens at the invitation of Hipparchus.[15] There he continued his activity as instructor of choruses and composer after the end of tyranny (509 B.C.). Tradition made him a teacher of Pindar and a competitor not unworthy of Simonides, who supposedly defeated him in a dithyrambic contest. The memory of the rivalry between the two poets was still alive at the end of the fifth century. In the *Clouds*

25

(1353 ff.) Aristophanes refers to Simonides as the author of compositions in the old style no longer appreciated by young people, and in the *Wasps* (1410–11) he opposes Simonides to Lasus, the proponent of new musical ideas.

The fragment of Lasus (*PMG* fr. 702) says, "I sing of Demeter and of Kore, wife of Klymenos, intoning the sweet hymn on the low-roaring Aeolian harmonia."[16] That such an expression should occur in a verse by Lasus is in itself significant. It implies an entirely new way of understanding song composition. In fact, several sources (Ps.-Plut. *De mus.* 29; Theon Smyrn. p. 59, 4 Hiller; *Suda* s.v.) say that Lasus is responsible for fundamental musical innovations: the search for new tunings on the cithara, which would allow playing inner notes at smaller intervals—tone and semitone—than was customary for citharodes of the past; the introduction of new rhythms, which Lasus is supposed to have adapted for use in the dithyramb; the theoretical definition of the size of intervals; and the composition of the first treatise on music.

Lasus must have felt the need to modify cithara tuning and obtain intervals a semitone smaller in order to adjust the performance of the instrument to the characteristics of a new repertory. This hypothesis, likely in itself, is confirmed by an examination of the basic structures of Greek music, especially with regard to the melodic genera (*gene*). As I have said, the fundamental schema, comparable in importance to our octave, was the tetrachord, i.e., an ensemble of four contiguous sounds, whose extreme notes were at an interval of a fourth (two tones plus a semitone). The placing of internal intervals could vary according to the position one would attribute to the two inner notes. If the intervals were placed in ascending order—semitone, tone, tone—the tetrachord belonged to the diatonic *genos;* if the succession was semitone, semitone, tone-and-a-half, the tetrachord was of the chromatic *genos;* if, finally, the succession was quarter tone, quarter tone, two tones, the *genos* of the tetrachord was the enharmonic. This last genus was supposedly invented by Olympus, the ancient Phrygian aulete (Ps.-Plut. *De mus.* 11), and was originally used only in auletic and aulodic compositions, since to raise the value of a note by a quarter tone was easy only on the aulos, by partially closing a hole. We must presume, therefore, that Lasus modified the tuning of the cithara for the purpose of playing on it the enharmonic tetrachord and executing such motifs originally meant for the aulos as the dithyrambic melodies of the Phrygian harmonia. Lasus was, of course, a citharode and an instructor of dithyrambic choruses.

Theon of Smyrna gives credit for the assignment of numerical values for the ratio between two sounds at a certain interval to both Lasus and the Pythagorean Hippasus of Metapontum (Diels-Kranz, *Vors.* 1:110, 3 ff.). These theorists are said to have identifed 2:1 as the ratio between two sounds at the interval of an octave, 3:2 as the ratio corresponding to the interval of a fifth, and 4:3 to the interval of a fourth. The attribution of this discovery to the one or the other is not important, at least for our present purposes. It is significant, however, that Lasus and the Pythagoreans, for different reasons, should have simultaneously felt the need to give a mathematical basis to the theory of musical intervals.

Pythagoras (ca. 560–470 B.C.) had left his native city of Samos at the time of Polycrates. After traveling for a long time in the East, where according to tradition he became familiar with Egyptian and Caldaean science (Diog. Laert. *Vitae phil.* 8, 3), he founded at Croton in Magna Graecia a school to which he gave the character of a religious sect, obliging his disciples to follow strict rules of life.[17] Pythagoras and his followers devoted a great deal of attention to acoustical and musical phenomena. They regarded consonances—especially of a fourth, fifth, and octave—as models of that harmony, conceived of as an accord or equilibrium of different elements, which they equated with the human soul or with the ordering principle of the universe. The assignment of the numerical ratios that are at the basis of musical concordances was for the Pythagoreans the starting point for discovering the laws which governed both the feelings of the soul and the movements of the universe. They arrived at these results experimentally, through the monochord, whose invention was attributed to Pythagoras himself.

The method, formulations, and goals of Pythagorean acoustical research had a decisive influence on the direction of all subsequent speculative work in the field of music. Damon and, after him, Plato and Aristotle especially, advanced the study of the effects of music on the human soul. Aristoxenus, on the other hand, and all the scholars of the Hellenistic and Roman periods—with the exception perhaps of the Epicurean theorists—took as the basis for their research the physical and mathematical principles embodied in Pythagorean doctrine.

Simonides, Bacchylides, and Pindar

Simonides, Bacchylides, and Pindar, the three great choral poets of the fifth century, lived during the transition period between the archaic age of the nomes and the classical age of the harmoniae, between a ritual conception of music and a new approach—which we might call secular—toward understanding traditional musical values. Simonides and his nephew Bacchylides were originally from Ceos, an island off the Ionian coast. Pindar came from Cynocephalae in Boeotia, which belonged to the Aeolian linguistic area. They practiced their profession in many cities of Greece and Southern Italy, wherever a client requested their services as poets and instructors of choruses. The literary genre to which they especially devoted themselves was the epinician ode, that is, the song in honor of the victors in the Panhellenic Olympian, Pythian, Nemaean, and Isthmian games. The family or the city of the victorious athlete would commission the poet to compose a victory song, which would be performed by a chorus either at the place of the victory or during the celebrations held upon the athlete's return home.[18]

Simonides' compositions must not have differed from the melodic forms of the nomes. He is remembered as the author of partheneia, prosodia, and paeans in the traditional Dorian harmonia (Aristox. fr. 82 Wehrli). In Aristophanes' *Clouds* (1352 ff.) Pheidippides, a fashionable youth, refuses to sing the outdated songs of Simonides and Aeschylus; he prefers the modern tunes of Euripides instead.

Pindar's odes provide more specific information.[19] He mentions traditional nomes three times: "I must crown the victor with the Hippian nomos of the Aeolian song" (*Ol.* 1.100 ff.); "Look kindly upon the Castorian (nome) on the Aeolian strings, meeting the grace of the seven-string *phorminx*" (*P.* 2.69 ff.); and in a very fragmentary passage (fr. 128e Snell-Maehler), where he speaks of the *nomos Orthios Ialemos* but in a context that is unclear. Mentioned far more frequently are harmoniae to which the song must conform: the Dorian (*Ol.* 3.5; *P.* 8.20; etc.); the Aeolian (*N.* 3.79; fr. 191 Snell-Maehler), the Lydian (*Ol.* 5.19, 11.17, *N.* 4.45; etc.). It is significant also that both references to the nomes should be accompanied by reference to the Aeolian harmonia.

We may therefore conjecture Pindar's adherence to the new musical idea of the harmoniae. This hypothesis is to some extent confirmed by the testimony (*Schol.* Pind. *Ol.* 1:4, 12 ff. Drachmann) that Pindar was a disciple of the innovator Lasus. It would also be consistent with the poet's own statements with regard to the novelty of his song ("Praise old wine, but the flowers of hymns that are young," *Ol.* 9.48 ff., and "the new winged song," *I.* 5.63, to cite only two examples) if I am right in interpreting them not in a restricted sense, as pertinent solely to the content and rhythm of the poetic text, but globally, as relevant to the melodic element as well.[20] Moreover, the use of auloi and *phorminx* for accompanying the same tune—the so-called *synaulia*, which is attested for some Pindaric odes (cf., e.g., *Ol.* 3.8, 7.12, 10.94)—represents an innovation with respect to the traditional manner of executing lyric song. We receive the impression of a continuous search for new approaches within a traditional range and for harmonic coexistence of ancient and modern musical elements, as the reference to nomes and harmoniae in the same ode suggests. The poet reveals his versatility and his mastery of the full range of compositional styles, adopting whatever style suits the particular nature of his song.

The Musical Ideas of Damon

Under the influence of Lasus and perhaps also Pindar, a disciple of Lasus, Greek music assumed characteristics that marked a step forward in relation to past forms, even though the traditional melodies, the nomes, would still be performed in the fifth century. This first musical reform also favored instrumental virtuosity, especially in the playing of the aulos when accompanying the di-thyrambic song. According to Pseudo-Plutarch (*De mus.* 30), "After Lasus, aulos playing passed from the simple to more varied music. For in the old days, up to the time of the dithyrambic poet Melanippides [around 450 B.C.], the auletes used to be paid by the poets, since poetry held the first place [in the composition], and the auletes were subordinate to the chorus instructors; but later this practice was abandoned." Pronomus of Thebes, born around 475 B.C., improved the aulos technically in order to increase its performance potential (Athen. 14.631e). Opposition did occasion-ally assert itself against the soloistic licenses of the auletes, who could overpower the chorus they were supposed to accompany. Pratinas of Phlius, in a famous *hyporchema* (Athen. 14.617b–f = *PMG* fr. 708), calls the aulos to order by means of graphic images, exhorting it to respect, and defer to, song and dance:

> What uproar is this? What are these dances? What outrage hath as-sailed the altar of Dionysus with its loud clatter? Bromius is mine, he is mine! Mine is the right to sing, the right to raise a clatter as I speed over the mountains with the Naiads, even as the swan with its motley-plumed melody. 'Tis the song that is queen stablished by the Pierian Muse; but the flute must be second in the dance, for he is e'en a servant; let him be content to be leader in the revel only, in the fist-fights of tipsy youngsters raging at the front door. Beat back him who has the breath of a mottled toad, burn up in flames that spit-wasting, babbling rau-cous reed, spoiling melody and rhythm in its march, that hireling whose body is fashioned by an auger! Look at me! Here thou shalt have the proper tossing of hand and foot, thou ivy-tressed lord of tri-umphant dithyramb; hear now the Dorian dance-song that is mine. (trans. C. B. Gulick)

But the process of musical renewal did not come to a stop, al-though until the last decades of the fifth century innovation was largely restricted to the dithyramb.

It was in this climate of musical reform that Damon developed his thought. Damon was teacher and adviser of Pericles, and was sent into exile in 444–43 B.C., perhaps because he induced Peri-cles to build the Odeum (a roofed hall for singing performances) at enormous cost to the state treasury. He was an outstanding figure in Athenian culture; a few years before his exile, he had delivered in front of the Council of the Areopagus a speech in which he expounded his theories about the importance of music in education.[21] His doctrine is based on the fundamental principle of Pythagorean psychology, that there is an essential identity between the laws which regulate relations among sounds and the laws which regulate the behavior of the human soul. Music, therefore, can influence character, especially in the young and still malleable (fr. 7 Lasserre). Among various types of melodies and rhythms, one must identify those most capable of educating the young to virtue, wisdom, and justice (fr. 6 Lasserre). In defining and analyzing the harmoniae, Damon maintains that only the Dorian and the Phrygian have a positive paideutic function because they encourage valorous behavior in war and instill wisdom and moderation in peace. On the subject of rhythm Damon pursued a similar line of inquiry, except that here we do not know the results. We know only that he classified rhythms according to "genres" on the basis of the relation between strong and weak beats: he distinguished a "composite enoplian" of the mixed genre, even and double together, from the "dactyl" and the "heroon" (probably the hexameter) of the even genre, and from the "iamb" and the "trochee" of the double genre (fr. 16 Lasserre). A passage in the *Republic* (4.424c = fr. 14 Lasserre) attributes to Damon a statement about the relationship between music and society, which Plato himself will later reiterate and elaborate upon: new musical fashions should be avoided, lest one endanger the institutions and laws of the state.

Damon's position vis-à-vis the music of his time is clear and consistent. He accepted the innovations which in the sixth and fifth centuries had caused melody to evolve from the repetitive nomic form to the greater freedom of the harmonia, insofar as they had not essentially violated tradition. But beginning from the middle of the fifth century, dithyrambic poetry had attempted to free its melodic structure from traditional generic bonds by borrowing melodic forms from other poetic genres. In the face of this trend, Damon's attitude was one of staunch opposition, such as

Plato would later assume with regard to the poet-musicians of his time who attempted to subvert and confuse traditional melodies without regard for the poetic genre.

Damon's ideas wielded considerable influence in subsequent centuries. His theories about the *ethos* of the harmoniae with reference to education were accepted by Plato and Aristotle, and they therefore conditioned Hellenistic and Roman thinking on the subject.[22] The systematic classification of the harmoniae according to ethical, rather than formal, criteria served as the basis for later musical speculation. Because of the weight of authority attributed to him in Hellenistic and Roman musical doctrine, his rejection of any novelty outside tradition must have played a crucial role in determining the directions taken by musicologists who favored research on problems of musical ethics and mathematics over the study of musical practice in their time.

One should emphasize, moreover, that the idea of assigning to the various harmoniae an *ethos*—a character, that is—which emotionally affects the human soul in a positive or a negative way provides additional evidence that the meaning of the term *harmonia* cannot be restricted to "modal scale, disposition of the intervals in the scale of octave." This sense alone would not be sufficient to justify the psychagogic effects which, according to Damon, the different musical forms were capable of producing.

Fifth-Century Attic Drama

About the music of the earliest tragic and comic poets we possess only general information.[23] Phrynichus, victor of the tragic contest of 510 B.C. and producer of the *Phoenician Women* in 476 B.C., is said to have composed exceedingly sweet songs (Aristoph. *Birds* 750; *Wasps* 218 ff.), which he probably borrowed from the Ionic tradition and from the ritual melodies of Phrygia (Aristoph. *Birds* 746 ff.). More specific is the statement that neither Phrynichus nor Aeschylus used the chromatic genus (Ps.-Plut. *De mus.* 20), implying that they remained faithful to the diatonic and enharmonic genera of the Dorian and Phrygian traditions.

Aeschylus, born in 525 B.C. and a contemporary of Pindar, was active in Athens until 458. He then moved to Sicily, where he died in 456. The musical forms in his tragedies diverged not at all from the earliest nomes. In the *Frogs*, Aristophanes compares the musical styles of Aeschylus and Euripides: in the dispute between the two poets, Aeschylus is accused of composing melodies that are all alike (line 1250), and he is mocked on account of his monotonous use of the cithara in the accompaniment of lyric song (lines 1286 ff.). Euripides criticizes him for indiscriminately employing songs "built with citharodic nomes" (line 1281), and Dionysus, who intervenes in the argument, describes Aeschylus's tunes as melodies suited for "someone who draws water from a well" (line 1297), alluding perhaps to the continuous repetition of the same rhythmic pattern. Direct reference to the nomes can be found in Aeschylus's own tragedies: to the Ionian nome (*Suppl.* 69), the Ialemos (*Suppl.* 115; *Choeph.* 424), the Acute (*Sept.* 954), the Orthios (*Ag.* 1153). In a passage of the *Persians* (line 937), the words "Mariandynian lamentations" would refer, according to an ancient gloss (*Schol. Aesch. Pers.* 917), also to the accompanying instrument, the Mariandynian aulos. Asiatic in origin, it had a high pitch and a timbre of lament. All these passages refer to a kind of music which adhered to the schemes of traditional songs and which, at the end of the fifth century, in spite of its austere grandeur, could well be regarded as antiquated.

Certain considerations lead to the conclusion that Sophocles (496–405 B.C.) accepted the musical innovations we have discussed in connection with Lasus and Pindar. In Sophocles there is a greater variety of meter and rhythm than in Aeschylus. Unusual elsewhere in dramatic lyric is Sophocles' use of such choral passages as the *hyporchema* (*Schol.* Soph. *Ai.* 693), of monodic songs—real soloistic tunes—and of duets, and, finally, the use of Phrygian and dithyrambic melodies in addition to the Dorian and Mixolydian, more commonly employed in Attic drama (*Vita Soph.* 23). Also, Sophocles' increase of the size of the chorus from twelve to fifteen members (*Vita Soph.* 4; *Suda* s.v. "Sophocles") must have to some extent involved an interest in new effects of timbre and volume in the performance of lyric song. The ancients, it is said, admired the sweetness of Sophocles' melodies (cf. *Schol.* Aristoph. *Peace* 531).

The musical style of Euripides (482?–406 B.C.) requires more complex treatment. Extant are seventeen tragedies and a single satyr drama, all belonging to the period of the poet's maturity: the *Alcestis*, the earliest surviving play, was produced first in 438, and the *Iphigenia in Aulis* after his death. This substantial corpus reveals the evolution of Euripides' conception of the dramatic function of music. In his work music gradually loses its traditional function as the support for the poetic text and becomes instead a means of expressing dramatic moments, the emotions and the states of mind represented in the tragedy—a new role fulfilled especially by the actors' astrophic songs, which are free of the strophic responsion typical of choral odes. Monodies, which were rare and of limited extent in the tragedies of the first period, become ever more frequent and longer, making the tragedy equivalent to a downright melodrama with arias and duets.

This approach to theater did not immediately meet with the approval of audience and critics. The flood of music, from the chorus to the solo singers, found in Aristophanes a harsh and stubborn judge. In the *Frogs*, the comic poet expresses his violent disapproval (not devoid of mordant irony) when he makes Aeschylus say that Euripides' tunes reproduced "the songs of whores," "the sympotic songs of Meletus" (a mediocre poet, more famous as the accuser of Socrates), "the tunes for auloi of Caria, *threnoi*, dance music" (*Frogs* 1300 ff.). Euripides was, in other words, a frivolous "collector of Cretan monodies" (*Frogs* 849). In his polemic, Aristophanes berated Euripides for filling his plays with popular, heart-rending, and exotic songs, which were aimed only to appeal to the emotions of the audience and which defiled the solemn and austere character of the ancient harmonies. But this excessive and summary judgment was later undermined by developments in Hellenistic theater and by the popularity which Euripidean tragedy enjoyed from the fourth century B.C. on.

The New Dithyramb and the Reforms of Timotheus

In his last tragedies, Euripides had adopted the musical innovations made by the authors of dithyrambs and citharodic nomes—by Melanippides, Crexus, Phrynis, Cinesias, Philoxenus, and especially Timotheus of Miletus.[24] As we saw earlier in the discussion of Lasus and his contemporaries, the impulse to revitalize the dithyrambic genre had probably been impelled by the competitive spirit which prevailed among the poets participating in the Great Dionysia. The ten authors of the compositions presented each year were more and more stimulated to look for new styles of song and to break away from traditional forms. Around the middle of the fifth century Melanippides composed dithyrambs without strophic responsion (Aristot. *Rhet.* 3.1409b26 ff.). Crexus introduced into the dithyramb spoken dialogue and recitative accompanied by the aulos, equivalent to Archilochian *parakataloge* (Ps.-Plut. *De mus.* 28). Phrynis, who directed his innovative inclinations into the sphere of monodic music, used more than one harmonia in the same composition (Pherecr. fr. 145; 14 ff. Kock); being a skillful citharode, he reelaborated the nome of Terpander and transformed it into a virtuosic tune. Cinesias, one of the targets of Aristophanes' jokes (*Birds* 1377 ff.; *Lys.* 838 ff.; *Frogs* 153, 1437; *Eccl.* 330), altered the very essence of the dithyramb by introducing into it ornamental features entirely alien to the genre (Pherecr. fr. 145; 8 ff. Kock). Philoxenus also contributed to changing the nature of the dithyrambic song by mixing harmoniae and rhythms of different genres (Dion. Hal. *De comp. verb.* 19.131), and by including monodic songs in the cyclic chorus (Ps.-Plut. *De mus.* 30).

The most famous representative of this revolutionary musical school was Timotheus of Miletus (ca. 450–360 B.C.), who brought to completion the renovating process begun by his predecessors. He was a prolific composer of hymns, nomes, dithyrambs, and instrumental *prooimia*, and was himself a famous citharode (he had been a disciple of Phrynis). He increased to eleven the number of the strings on the cithara (Tim. *Pers.* 229 ff. *PMG*) in order to adapt its expressive potential to his virtuosic talents. He also revised the rhythmic structure of the citharodic nome by interweaving elements that were typical of the dithyrambic genre into a scheme which preserved the dactylic sequences of the old citharody, so as not to break completely with the past (Ps.-Plut. *De mus.* 4). Of a nome by Timotheus, the *Persians,* which narrates the battle between Greeks and Barbarians at Salamis, we possess a long fragment from a Berlin papyrus of the fourth century B.C. (*PMG* fr. 791), one of the most ancient that has been preserved.[25] Even though the papyrus is contemporary to, or only slightly later than, the composition of the nome, it bears no trace of a musical score—a fact which confirms the thesis that music began to be written down only in subsequent times. In the last part of the *Persians,* Timotheus talks about himself and his work, stating that he made the cithara more expressive "by the meters and rhythms of the eleven sounds" (lines 229–31), and claiming that he had opened "the secret coffer of the Muses of the many hymns" (lines 232–33). Increasing the number of strings evidently allowed him to perform within a single song melodies of the diatonic, enharmonic, and chromatic genera.[26]

The distinction between "meters" and "rhythms" in the passage cited above is a meaningful testimony of the new relationship between the structures of the poetic text and the measures of the musical beat. Previously, the time of execution was determined by the alternation of long and short syllables in the verbal text. Meter imposed itself as the rhythmic basis of the performance, as we saw at the beginning of this chapter, and rhythmic modulation conformed entirely to the metrical scheme of the text. The mimetic character of the "new music," on the other hand, required the greatest freedom of both rhythm and melody, so as to evoke effectively the variety of situations described in the text. In the *Persians,* the turmoil of battle and the confusion of defeat (lines 1–97) are followed by laments of the vanquished (lines 98–161), the despair of Xerxes (lines 162–95), and the joy of the victors (lines 196–201), in a succession of scenes full of pathetic and dramatic tension.

The originality and diversity of metrical schemes, lexical forms, and linguistic structures also attest to the search for mimetic expressiveness. Next to dactylic verses typical of the traditional nome (dactylic tetrameters, catalectic and acatalectic: $-\smile\smile-\smile\smile$ $-\smile\smile-$ and $-\smile\smile-\smile\smile-\smile\smile-\smile\smile$), we find choriambic dimeters ($-\smile\smile--\smile\smile-$) in all their possible variations, as well as iambic, trochaic, and cretic ($-\smile-$) meters underlining the different moments of the narrative. The normalized forms of the dimeter (the glyconic $\times\times-\smile\smile-\smile\overset{\smile}{-}$, and the pherecratean $\times\times-\smile\smile-\overset{\smile}{-}$) denote the last section of the poem, with the personal "seal" (*sphragis*). The use of daring neologisms, metaphors, and compound words; the search for phonic effects (alliterations and imitative harmonies); as well as characterization by means of the dialect expressions of the Barbarians speaking in the first person—all reveal the requirement of mimetically conforming the language to the different moments of the dramatic event.

Timotheus introduced to the dithyramb soloistic parts, passed from one harmonia to another and from one genus to another in continuous *metabolai* or modulations (Dion. Hal. *De comp. verb.* 19. 131). In a fragment the poet states resolutely: "I do not sing old things; my new compositions are better. Now Zeus is king, while Chronus once was; farewell to the old Muse!" There is a decisive and radical contrast between the new art and the traditional forms. Athenians did not at first approve unanimously of these new musical fashions. During the earlier period of his activity, Timotheus found himself at the center of a lively dispute (cf. Plut. *An seni sit respublica gerenda* 23). And this is reflected also in Aristophanes' anti-Euripidean tirades (Euripides had supported and encouraged Timotheus at the beginning of his career). In a fragment of Pherecrates' *Cheiron* (Ps.-Plut. *De mus.* 30 = fr. 145 Kock), the melodies of Timotheus are called "ant-hills of abnormal notes," with a metaphor analogous to that used by Aristophanes ("ant-runs," *Thesm.* 100) for the tunes of Agathon, the tragedian who, like Euripides, shared the innovating propensities of the dithyrambic poets.[27]

A few decades later, when the "new music" had become established, Plato voiced the very criticisms and accusations the conservatives had leveled against the poet from Miletus. In the *Republic* (3.397c ff.; 10.595a ff.) he discusses the ethical function of art in his ideal state and flatly rejects the "new" mimetic and expressionistic music on the grounds that it stimulates emotions and passions upsetting to a man's rational equilibrium. At the ethical level, the narrative type of expression is for Plato better than the imitative type, in which speeches are rendered in the first person and the author tends to identify with the protagonist of the reported action:

> One of them [i.e., the narrative style] involves little change and variety; when the words have been fitted to a suitable musical mode (*harmonia*) and rhythm, the recitation can keep almost to the same mode and rhythm throughout, the modulations required being slight. The other, on the contrary, involves every sort of variation and demands the use of all the modes and rhythms there are.—Quite true—Now, all writers and composers fall into one or other of the extreme styles, or a mixture of both. What shall we do? Are we to admit into our commonwealth one or other of the extreme styles, or the mixed one, or all three?—If my judgement is to prevail, the simple one, which serves to represent a fine character. (Plato *Rep.* 3.397b–d; trans. Cornford)

One is therefore called on to reject any form of variation or modulation of harmoniae and rhythms that is typical of imitative music. Music must always conform to the changes of character in the situations that are represented.

> Suppose . . . that an individual clever enough to assume any character and give imitations of anything and everything should visit our country and offer to perform his compositions, we shall bow down before a being with such miraculous powers of giving pleasure; but we shall tell him that we are not allowed to have any such person in our commonwealth; we shall crown him with fillets of wool, anoint his head with myrrh, and conduct him to the borders of some other country. (Plato *Rep.* 3.398a; trans. Cornford)

But the revisionary artistic tendencies had already asserted themselves. Composers were freed from the restrictions of musical genres and established a new relationship between text and melody, the latter endowed with absolute predominance. As the musical score became more complex, performances could no longer be entrusted to simple amateurs, but, rather, required the skill and

the vocal and instrumental virtuosity of professionals. Since chorus singers did not have the technical preparation of virtuosi, the
role of the chorus was diminished in drama as well. This new
approach to musical performance is announced clearly by the
author of the *Problems* attributed to Aristotle:

> Why are not the tunes called nomes arranged in antistrophes, while
> other choric songs are? Is it because nomes are delivered by profes-
> sional artists, and, as their function was to imitate action and sustain
> them, their song was long and took many forms? The songs, then,
> conformed to the imitation in the same way as the words and varied
> continually. In fact it was necessary to imitate by the tune even more
> than by the words. For the same reason the dithyrambs, once they had
> become imitative, were no longer antistrophic, as they had previously
> been. The reason is, that in the old days free citizens acted in the
> choruses; hence it was difficult for a number to sing together as
> professional artists, so that they performed their song in the enhar-
> monic scale; for it is easier for one person alone to execute variations
> than for a number, and for a professional artist than for those who have
> to preserve the character of the music. That is why they composed
> simpler chants for the latter. The antistrophe composition is a simple
> thing; for it is composed in a single rhythm and in a single metre. It is
> for the same reason that songs performed on the stage are not anti-
> strophic, while those performed by the chorus are; for the actor is a
> professional artist and imitator, but the chorus is less capable of filling
> an imitative role. (Ps.-Aristot. *Probl.* 19.15; trans. W. S. Hett)

Yet Aristophanes himself, a contemporary of Timotheus and an
opponent of the new music, in the course of his career as dramatic
author came to reduce considerably the number and extent of the
choral parts (to the point even of giving up the parabasis in the last
of his comedies), and increased instead the lyric songs of the
actors.

Unlike Plato, who had banned from his ideal city any form of
mimetic art, Aristotle in the last chapters of his *Politics* (8.1339b10
ff.) gives a substantially positive evaluation of the music of his
time.[28] He states that musical education should provide a man
with dignified enjoyment in moments of rest, enhance the development of a morally irreprehensible character, and lead him to

wisdom. The goals of music, therefore, do for Aristotle include the pursuit of pleasure, so that all melodic types, even those which Plato forbade in his ideal state, achieve positive recognition: "We must permit musicians who are competing before an audience of the baser sort to use a baser sort of music which corresponds to their audience" (Aristot. *Pol.* 8.1342a26 ff.; trans. Barker). Aristotle goes on to say that songs that greatly trouble the soul through the imitation of violent passions, have the beneficial effect of cathartic release. All melodies should be used, each for its special purpose.

The Dorian and Lydian *harmoniae* are the most suitable, Aristotle thinks, for the ethical upbringing of the young. The Phrygian mode, approved of by Plato, Aristotle regards as too excited and orgiastic. Musical education is supposed to provide the means for judging the beauty of songs and for enjoying them righteously. It should be a form of teaching that prepares one for listening rather than for direct performance. Here Aristotle is taking into account the reality of his time, which had considerably limited musical amateurism. With regard to professional activity, however, he maintains an attitude of detachment and disapproval, insofar as it turns those who practice it into "vulgar mechanics" (8.1340b20 ff.). This statement may partially explain the lack of interest on the part of theorists for the technique and practice of musical composition and performance, which in Hellenistic times had become the apanage of professionals.

The Hellenistic Age

The "revolution" begun by Timotheus and the dithyrambic poets of the fifth century affected the musical culture and institutions of the Greeks and the Romans down to the end of the ancient world. Traditional forms of musical performance underwent notable transformations: in comedy musical and dance elements all but disappeared in the end, except for a few lyric songs assigned to the actors, as in the *Theophoroumene* of Menander (p. 146 Sandbach); the chorus appeared only in the intervals between acts, performing material that bore no relation to the subject matter of the play, in this following a practice already instaurated in tragedy by Agathon (Aristot. *Poet.* 18.1456a30).

Beginning in the fourth century B.C., a new type of show became popular, the recital by a virtuoso (*tragodos*) who would sing and mime with instrumental accompaniment either original texts or, more frequently, texts transcribed from the dramatic repertoire of the fifth century.[29] These were almost always taken from anthologic prompt-books containing passages from one or more tragedies. A few meaningful exemplars have been preserved: the *PLeid.* inv. 510 (middle of the third century B.C.) contains a selection of lyric songs from Euripides' *Iphigenia in Aulis* along with the musical score. Music began to be written down in the fourth and third centuries precisely because traditional melodic forms were no longer being followed. As we have already seen, however, the use of notation never spread outside the narrow circle of professional actors and musicians.

Cult hymns and lyric poems, both monodic and choral, designed for the various communal events, continued to be executed in public performances. I refer especially to the two Delphic hymns of the second century B.C. (see above, p. 21), composed in paeons and cretics and structured along the melodic lines of traditional music.

The rhapsodes, professional singers who in Hellenistic times were often associated with theatrical companies, sang to musical accompaniment texts—such as Homer, Hesiod, Archilochus, Mimnermus, and Phocylides (Ath. 14.620c)—which for the most part were originally meant for recitation and declamation. Numerous inscriptions document the activity of poets and musicians who obtained prizes and honors in several Greek cities for their artistic performances.[30]

Historians and scholars of Greek music mention no famous composer after Timotheus, and name only virtuosic singers and instrumentalists. Audiences admired technical accomplishment and rewarded those who displayed it with victory in the musical competitions held at solemn festivals, as celebratory inscriptions attest, in many cities of the Hellenic area, such as Orchomenus,

Thespiae, Teos, and Chios. At Delphi, theatrical contests and competitions among solo singers took place at the *Soteria,* a festival instituted in 279 B.C. to commemorate the defeat of the Galatians, who had attempted to sack the sanctuary of Apollo. These events attracted virtuoso companies ("corporations of Dionysiac artists") from every part of Greece.[31] These companies—which might include tragic and comic actors (*tragodoi* and *komodoi*), citharodes, aulodes, chorus singers, instructors, and rhapsodes—changed their membership according to the demands of the repertoire. They performed in all the most important centers of the Hellenized world and, in the Hellenistic and Roman periods, propagated knowledge of the dramatic texts of the classical tradition, albeit modified and adapted to suit new theatrical practices.

The Hellenistic age also saw the development of schools which prepared young people to a specific musical activity. An inscription from Teos (*CIG* 2:3088) provides information on the disciplines that were taught: from citharistic and citharodic technique to rhythmic and melic practice, to comic and tragic recitation, these schools offered a curriculum that insured the continuity of theatrical and musical education.

The new approach to theater, drawing on music of diverse color and timbre according to the nature of the texts performed, resulted in the more frequent use of the *synaulia,* that is, the accompaniment by string and wind instruments playing together. This practice, already attested in Pindar, led in Roman imperial times to the establishment of real orchestras. Seneca (*Ep.* 84.10), speaking of a musical performance, declares himself impressed by the number of the chorus singers ("there are more singers in our concerts than there were spectators in the old theaters") and of the players, who filled the whole stage and even the top of the cavea. And yet, the simultaneous use of many instruments did not result in the kind of harmony and polyphony that characterize modern music. That phenomenon remained absent even after the invention by Ctesibius of Alexandria (third century B.C.) of the water-organ (*hydraulis*), an instrument very similar to modern organs which utilized water pressure to supply air to a set of pipes.

Music Theory

During all of Hellenistic and Roman history, from Aristoxenus on, theoreticians continued in the footsteps of Pythagoras and Damon, and paid little attention to the musical developments of their own time. They studied the mathematical value of intervals and their arrangement within the tetrachords, they defined the various systems formed by the union of two or more tetrachords, and they continued to discuss the problems of musical *ethos*.

Since in the Hellenistic and Roman ages archaic and classical music was no longer performed, the precise notion of *harmonia* as it had been formulated in the period from Lasus to Aristotle (see above, p. 26) was also forgotten. The term *harmonia* in the Pythagorean tradition from Philolaus on (cf. Nicomachus *Ench.* 9, p. 252, 3 Jan) restrictively defined the octave interval, within which the sounds of the tuning of the cithara were comprised. In Aristoxenus, on the other hand, it indicated the enharmonic *genos,* only one of the characteristics, that is, which in the past contributed to defining the harmoniae—in particular the Phrygian. The names of the ancient harmoniae—Dorian, Aeolian, Phrygian, Lydian, Ionian—were used also for indicating and distinguishing the *tonoi* or *tropoi.* These were scales which differed in relative pitch, and which transposed within the Perfect Immutable System of two octaves all the aspects which the four tetrachords conjoined two by two could assume. If the position of the different *tonoi* and *tropoi* and their mutual relationships were still not well defined at the time of Aristoxenus (*Harm.* 2.37 ff., p. 46, 17 Da Rios), in Roman times, each of them found its own position in the Perfect System and was described in the tables of notation (cf. Alypius *Isag.* 1 ff., pp. 367 ff. Jan).

To the scales, so defined, those same characteristics of musical *ethos* were attributed which Damon and his followers had identified in the homonymous *harmoniai* (Ptol. *Harm.* 2.7, p. 58, 7 ff. Düring). There were those, however, like the anonymous author of *PHibeh* 1.13[32] and the Epicurean Philodemus of Gadara (first century B.C.), who did not recognize the ethical value of music.

Philodemus took a position against the Stoic Diogenes of Babylon by maintaining that, in *mousike,* melody and rhythm without words cannot have ethical function (*De mus.* 4, pp. 64 ff. Kemke).

The first musicologist of the Hellenistic age was Aristoxenus of Tarentum, a disciple of Aristotle. His works provided the foundation for all subsequent musical theory.[33] In his *Harmonic Elements,* after defining his area of inquiry (the study of intervals, tetrachords, and systems), he identifies the elements of melody and the genera (diatonic, enharmonic, and chromatic) of the tetrachords. Aristoxenus maintained that the calculation of the relationships among the different sounds and of the measure of the intervals is not sufficient to explain musical phenomena and to indicate the characteristics of the correct composition. For the comprehension of music, the listener needs ear, intellect, and memory, which will together permit him to perceive the relation among notes in their succession (*Harm.* 2.31 ff., p. 40, 12 ff. Da Rios). Although Aristoxenus recognized the value of the mathematical research initiated and developed by the Pythagoreans, he emphasized the role of sense perception for judging musical phenomena that are dynamic rather than static.

In the third book of the *Harmonic Elements,* Aristoxenus undertakes closer analysis of the tetrachords, particularly with respect to the definition of the genera, and considers the different forms which tetrachords can assume according to the placement of the two inner notes. His work does not, however, contain any mention of the harmoniae.

In the *Rhythmic Elements,* the work in which he considers the chronic values of the poetic text in the musical performance, Aristoxenus defines the different rhythmic genres according to the mathematical ratio between the duration of strong (down) beats and of weak (up) beats: even ($1:1$ ratio), double ($2:1$), and hemiolion ($3:2$). The epitritic genre ($4:3$) is regarded by Aristoxenus as arhythmic (*Rhythm.* p. 25, 14 ff. Pighi); Aristides Quintilianus disagrees with him on this point (*De mus.* 1.14, p. 34, 13 ff. Winnington-Ingram) and, albeit with some reservations (*De mus.* 1.14, p. 33, 30 W.-I.), places this genre on the same level as the other three.

According to Aristoxenus, rhythmic analysis must also rely on aural perception (*aisthesis;* cf. *Rhythm.* p. 17, 8 ff.; 17, 28 ff.; 18, 23 ff.; 19, 26 ff., etc., Pighi). His discussion does not therefore concern the metrical structure of the verse, which is determined in a fixed manner by the quantity of the syllables; it focuses, rather, on the rhythmic configuration that poetry assumes at the moment of musical performance, which from the time of Timotheus was no longer linked to the temporal values of the verbal text.

Later treatises on music display some originality, not so much in the definitions and theoretical formulations, however, which follow for the most part Pythagorean and Aristoxenic schemes, as in the way they examine the educational value of music and, in general, explore the relationship between music and philosophy. A work valuable for the completeness and quality of the information it contains is the *De musica* by Aristides Quintilianus, most often regarded as belonging to the second century, though a different interpretation of the chronological data assigns him to the fourth century.[34] In the first book, after defining music and its components, the author summarizes the principles of music theory according to Aristoxenian schemes but from a broader viewpoint. He considers in general the relationship between melody and poetic text (*De mus.* 1.12, p. 28, 8 ff. W.-I.), and includes tables of musical notation. In the chapters dealing with rhythm and poetic meter (1.13 ff., p. 31, 3 ff. W.-I.), Aristides Quintilianus discusses the so-called *symplekontes,* namely, those whose analysis had not discriminated between rhythmic and metrical schemes, since in archaic and classical musical practice down to the time of Timotheus the two used to coincide. Aristides distinguishes this older theory from that developed by metricologists and rhythmicologists, who focused, respectively, on the metrical form of the text and on its rhythmical application in song.

In spite of the fact that the theoretical formulations of Aristides are not substantially new with respect to older rhythmic and metrical doctrines, his work stands out for its clear and systematic exposition. It also examines rhythmic structures such as epitritic rhythms (*De mus.* 1.14, p. 33, 30 ff. W.-I.), compound and mixed rhythms (*De mus.* 1.14, p. 34, 19 ff. W.-I.), and irrational rhythms

(1.17, p. 37, 24 ff. W.-I.), namely rhythms for which a constant ratio between strong and weak beats cannot be identified (1.14, p. 33, 21–22 W.-I.). Aristides Quintilianus's rhythmic doctrine is more sophisticated than Aristoxenus's and agrees with the anonymous rhythmic treatise of a papyrus of the third century (*POxy.* 9 + 2687), which examines the possible rhythmic applications of cretic, choriambic (– ᴗᴗ–), and dactylic meters. This is a text which its editors have attributed to Aristoxenus, but which is certainly the work of an author who has merely adopted the technical terminology and vocabulary of Aristides Quintilianus.[35]

In the second book of the rhythmic treatise Aristides considers the paideutic function of music and, in general, the effects that different types of music have on the human soul. Early on in the first book Aristides had stated that dialectic and rhetoric can benefit the soul only if they find it already purified by music (*De mus.* 1.1, p. 2, 3 ff. W.-I.). In the first chapters of the second book he defines music as the leading discipline for the education of the irrational element of the soul, assigning it to a position of primacy akin to that held by philosophy for the rational element (*De mus.* 2.3, p. 54, 27 ff. W.-I.). *Mousike*—intended as the union of word, melody, and dance—is the most effective of the arts for education. Painting and sculpture have limited effects because they present to the sight only a static representation of reality; poetry without melody and dance affects the soul through hearing, but cannot arouse pathos or lead the soul into conformity with the subjects treated. *Mousike*, on the other hand, by educating through word, melody, and dance, offers a mimetic representation of actions founded on rhythm. It acts through hearing and sight, realizing the highest degree of mimesis in a dynamic, rather than static, manner (*De mus.* 2.4, p. 56, 6 ff. W.-I.). Aristides Quintilianus, unlike Philodemus, admits to the existence of an *ethos* also for pure melody (*De mus.* 1.12, p. 30, 20 W.-I.), but he regards the combination of poetry, melody, and dance as the most accomplished form of art and, at the same time, the one most useful to education, because of the complementary functioning of each of its elements. The debate between those who denied the ethical value of music and considered melody and rhythm mere instruments of pleasure

(Philodemus) and those who attributed to music a primary function in the sphere of education (Aristides Quintilianus) had moralistic and rationalistic motives essentially analogous to those which many centuries later would be at the root of all the polemics on the relationship between music and poetry, in particular with regard to melodrama in the Italian and French cultures of the seventeenth and eighteenth centuries.[36]

Aristides Quintilianus (in *De mus.* 2.4 ff.) maintains that in performance the noble and virile features of thought and speech, as well as of melody and rhythm, must be held up for imitation. The Platonic origin of these principles is self-evident. But in the *De musica* we find the echo of other doctrines as well—Neoplatonic, Neopythagorean, Peripatetic, and Stoic. This is true especially of the third book, in which Aristides Quintilianus considers the relationship and analogy between the nature of the cosmos and the nature of man, between the music of the celestial spheres and earthly music.[37]

Elements of Neopythagorean and Neoplatonic cosmology also appear in the *De institutione musica* of Severinus Boethius (fifth century), especially in the distinction the author makes between *musica mundana, musica humana,* and *musica instrumentorum.* The first is the harmony of the universe which originates from the movement of the heavens and the stars and cannot be perceived by the human ear. The second is the harmony which allows the coexistence and mutual adaptation in humankind of the bodily and spiritual element. The third is the music of voices and instruments (*De inst. mus.* 1.2, p. 187, 18 ff. Friedlein).

Three

Roman Music

The Origins. Theater in the Third and Second Centuries B.C.

n the course of the third century B.C., Greek influence on
Roman culture became increasingly evident, a result of the
more frequent contacts between Rome and southern Italy, especially after Rome's victory against Tarentum and the First
Punic War. But Rome and Latium had maintained close relations with the Greek world ever since the city's foundation, a fact
demonstrated by the recovery of Submycenaean, Protocorinthian,
and Geometric pottery in different areas of the region.[1] Greek
civilization had also penetrated central Italy through the mediation of the Etruscans, who exerted a decisive influence on the
formation of Roman civil and religious institutions in the regal
period.

We know that forms of both monodic and choral ritual song
developed in Rome and Latium, but of the early musical forms no
direct or indirect evidence has survived.[2] All that remains are a few
fragments of song texts and fairly vague indications as to the
manner of their performance. The texts include sacral poems
(*Carmen Fratrum Arvalium, Carmen Saliare*) whose origins can be
traced back to the time of the first Roman kings; convivial songs

that are epic-historical in subject (*carmina convivialia*) and were accompanied by the *tibia* (an instrument equivalent to the Greek aulos); songs in honor of victorious generals (*carmina triumphalia*); and funerary lamentations (*neniae*).

Until the fourth century B.C. Roman theatrical performances displayed characteristics typical of dramatic performances among all primitive peoples: their recurrence was determined by the rhythm of agricultural tasks, motivated by ritual reasons, and founded on improvisation. Song and dance would accompany the jocular and often mordant jibes which the actors exchanged with the spectators (*Fescennini*); the production of country farces (*Atellanae*) left the protagonists free to improvise at will. In 364 B.C. *ludi scenici* were established in the hope of stopping a plague then afflicting the city: Etruscan actors (*ludiones*) danced to the sound of the tibia. These were imitated by the Roman youths, who added to the dance a rhythmically varied song on a tune played by the tibicen; they were given the name of *histriones* from *ister*, who among the Etruscans designated the dancer; their compositions were called *saturae* (Livy 7.2.3 ff.).

Improvised performances of this kind were popular in Rome until the middle of the third century B.C., when the occupation of southern Italy and Sicily after the First Punic War brought Romans into direct and continuous contact with Greek theatrical productions. The traditional dramatic forms were then replaced by the production of tragedies and comedies which were performed in Latin but whose structure and subject matter were borrowed from the Greek classical repertory, especially from Euripides and such poets of New Comedy as Menander, Diphilus, and Philemon. The first author in this new period of Roman theater was Livius Andronicus, a Greek from Tarentum who was brought to Rome as a slave and later freed. He led the way for such other poets as Naevius, Ennius, Plautus, Caecilius Statius, Pacuvius, Terence, and Accius, who during the third and second centuries B.C. were the protagonists of Roman cultural life.

The Greek classical repertoire had become known in Italy mainly through the productions of the Dionysiac artists, who had established companies in the most important cities of Magna

Graecia. As has already been mentioned, however, the prompt-books of these actors did not respect the original structure and integrity of the classical texts but, rather, modified them by cutting and moving whole passages, or by replacing passages with others taken from different works. Roman authors, especially the comic poets, behaved similarly with regard to the Greek originals which they translated into Latin. They used the technique of the *contaminatio*, which consisted precisely in introducing into the plot of a specific Greek comedy entire scenes taken from other Greek comedies by the same or by other Greek authors. In the subdividing of recited and sung parts (*deverbia* and *cantica*), they would depart from the Greek text and turn into song verses which in the original were meant for recitation. This happens, for example, in the *Medea* of Ennius and in the *Plocium* of Caecilius Statius. Greek virtuosi followed a similar practice when they put into music tragic passages in iambic trimeters, a meter previously reserved for recitation (as in *POsl.* 1413, of the first and second century).[3]

In these theatrical reelaborations music held a place of considerable importance. In tragedy, sung parts—solos and duets—alternated with spoken dialogue. The evidence for this consists in the extant fragments in lyric meter and in the testimony (assuming it refers to tragic performances) that Livius Andronicus, toward the end of his career as a composer and actor, reserved for himself on the stage the performance of speeches and mimetic action and entrusted the singing to a younger soloist (Livy 7.2.8 ff.). We cannot, on the other hand, maintain with certainty that Roman tragedy normally included choral songs, even though in a few plays some parts were given to the chorus (cf. Ennius *Iphig.* 183–90, pp. 44–45 Ribbeck; Pac. *Niptra* 259–62, p. 126 Ribbeck; Pompon. *inc. fab.* 5–11, p. 268 Ribbeck). In fact, the orchestra, which in the Greek theater was reserved to the chorus, was in the Roman theater occupied by the most distinguished spectators. A solo performed by the tibicen would often introduce the show, and at the first notes the most experienced among the audience would be able to recognize the tragedy, even before the title was announced (Cicero *Acad. Pr.* 2.7.20).

Also in comedy, as the meters of Plautus and Terence indicate, the *cantica* frequently alternated with the *deverbia*.[4] The predominance of parts sung by soloists over spoken passages all but eliminated the need for the chorus in the function of lyric intermezzo. Instrumental pieces could, rather, be inserted between acts, as in the *Pseudolus* of Plautus (line 573a: *tibicen vos interibi hic delectaverit*). Songs were generally accompanied by *tibiae*, the double auloi. The stage directions of Terence's comedies specify the type of instrument employed in each case: *tibiae pares,* of equal length; *tibiae impares,* which probably played at an octave interval from one another; *tibiae sarranae,* or Phoenician, Oriental *auloi.* The name of the tibicen, who was also the author of the pieces, is also recorded.

Unfortunately, of the melodies of Latin theater nothing has remained, nor has any information come down to us about their characteristics. Cicero (*Leges* 2.15.39), in connection with the music of Livius Andronicus and Naevius, merely speaks of *iucunda severitas,* austerity not devoid of pleasantness.

The Late Republic. The Empire

In 146 B.C., with the capture of Corinth, the Romans occupied the whole of Greece. The victors deprived the defeated Greeks of their freedom, but opened the doors of their own city to Greek culture. Men of letters, rhetors, artists, actors, and musicians came from Greece in great numbers and found in Rome the conditions most favorable for their activities. Music became in this period a subject studied by young men and even by young women of the upper classes (Macrobius *Saturnalia* 3.14.4 ff., pp. 196 ff. Willis). Greek teachers and performers became ever more greatly honored and appreciated. But the excesses of this Hellenizing fashion also provoked some reaction. This is reflected in the words of Scipio Aemilianus (Macr. *Sat.* 3.14.7, pp. 196 ff. Willis) and of Cicero (*Leg.* 2.15.39), who miss the simplicity of the tunes by Livius Andronicus and Naevius. Conservatives even imposed restrictions on the performances of the Greek virtuosi and on the use of instruments other than the tibia (edict of the censors Lucius Caecilius Metellus Delmaticus and Cn. Domitius Ahenobarbus, of 115 B.C.).[5]

Nothing, however, could blunt the growing popularity of the music imported from Greece.

Nor did the Romans stake out for themselves original theoretical positions, but seemed content to follow the lead of the Greeks. Varro's *De musica,* which constituted the seventh book of his encyclopedia (*Disciplinae*), is the first Latin treatise on music. No part of it has been preserved, but if the works of Censorinus (*De die nat.* 12.1 ff., pp. 29 ff. Jahn), Martianus Capella (*De nupt. Phil. et Merc.* 9.922 ff., pp. 490 ff. Dick), Cassiodorus (*Institut.* 2.5, pp. 142 ff. Mynors), and Macrobius (*Comm. ad Somn. Scip.* 2, 3, 4 ff., pp. 104 ff. Willis), refer in particular to this treatise, we have some idea of its content. It must have included not only the exposition of the musical theory proper but also an analysis of the relationship between the laws of harmony and those which regulate the equilibrium of the soul and of the universe, as well as reflections on the paideutic, medical, and magical effects of music, a description of the musical instruments, and a history of Greek and Roman music.[6] Varro dealt with music also in his *Saturae Menippeae:* the subject matter of the *Asinus ad lyram* (pp. 188 ff. Bolisani) is the teaching of music and the effects music has on listeners ("oftentimes, at the frequent variations of the tones of the tibia, the thoughts of all the spectators change, their souls leap"; fr. 17, p. 192 Bolisani). In the *Parmenon* (pp. 204 ff. Bolisani) the imitators of Greek rhythms and melodies are derided. Varro's work eclectically synthesized the principles of the Pythagorean, Platonic, Aristotelian, and Aristoxenian musical theory. In conjunction with the Greek texts of the imperial period, such as the *De musica* of Aristides Quintilianus, it doubtless provided the foundation for all the subsequent musicological literature.

Comedy and tragedy lost their positions of prominence on the Roman stage after Terence and Accius, owing to the dearth of authors capable of instilling vitality and interest into these dramatic genres. The old plays continued to be produced on special occasions: the funerary games that were held in 44 B.C. after the murder of Julius Caesar included a performance of Pacuvius's *Armorum judicium* (Suet. *Caes.* 84). About ten years earlier (55 B.C.), Accius's *Clutemnestra* had inaugurated the theater of Pompey.

In Rome, no less than in Greece, audiences seemed to reserve their interest for the performances of virtuosi, *comoedi* and *tragoedi*, rather than for the quality of the texts staged. Personalities like Roscius, whom Cicero mentions more than once as an actor and comic singer (*De orat*. 1.60; *Ad fam*. 9.22), or like Aesopus, a *tragoedus* named with Roscius by Quintilian (*Inst. or*. 11.3.111), must have enjoyed a considerable renown among Roman audiences.

Star worship and admiration for the virtuosity of the actors partly account for the increasing popularity in the first century B.C. of mime and pantomimes and other new types of show which centered around the performance of a soloist. The mime, a burlesque farce or comic-satiric play, engaged on the stage an actor who through speech, gesture, and sometimes dance to the sound of the tibia, realistically interpreted an event of daily life or parodied a mythological story. Pantomime was created in 22 B.C. by Pilas of Cilicia (Hieron. *Chron*. 27, p. 437 Migne), and consisted in the mimetic performance by solo dancers of scenes from myth and history. Musical accompaniment was provided by the chorus and by an orchestra of tibiae, citharae, pipes, and such percussion instruments as the *scabella*, struck with the foot, and cymbals (cf. Luc. *De saltat*. 68; Ovid. *Remed. amor*. 753–56). The music which accompanied these shows probably had the same mimetic character as the compositions designed for the performance of *comoedi* and *tragoedi*, since it functioned in an analogous way to comment on and connote the pathos of the dramatic actions.

Concerts were frequently given by imposing choral groups and large orchestras similar to those in pantomime performances, often reinforced by the instruments of military music—the *tuba, lituus, bucina, cornu* (cf. Sen. *Ep*. 84). Making a showing on other occasions was the water organ, or some other fairly unusual instruments, such as the cithara "as large as a chariot" mentioned by Ammianus Marcellinus (*Histories* 14.6.18, 1:21 Gardthausen).

In the imperial period, singers, dancers, and instrumentalists poured into Rome from Greece and other parts of the empire: from Egypt (cf. Propertius 4.8.39 ff.), Syria (Horace's *ambubaiae*, cf. *Satires* 1.2.1), Spain (the dancers of Gades, famous for their lascivious dances; cf. Martial *Epigr.* 6.71.1 ff.).[7] This phenomenon, which coincided with the massive immigration of provincials and slaves that deeply altered the demographics of the city, determined the formation of a diverse musical environment and the coexistence of heterogeneous forms of expression. Perhaps as a reaction to the perceived corruption of the Greco-Roman musical culture, some of the emperors, who were also good amateur performers or at least competent listeners, attempted to impart new luster to the ancient soloistic genres, such as citharody and citharistic music. Nero, a disciple of the Greek Terpnus, instituted musical contests and participated personally in citharodic competitions in Italy and Greece (Suet. *Nero* 20 ff.). Vespasian, on the occasion of the reopening of the theater of Marcellus, engaged the *tragodos* Apollinaris and the citharodes Terpnus and Diodorus for fees, in spite of his proverbial parsimony (Suet. *Vespasian* 19). Hadrian, who boasted of being a skillful citharode and singer (*Vita Hadr.* 15.9, 1:16 Hohl), patronized the citharode Mesomedes and supported musical study. But the audience's predilection for the most extraordinary and spectacular forms of musical performance never ceased. In 284 the emperor Carinus organized a concert with a hundred trumpet players, a hundred horn players, and two hundred tibicens (*Vita Carini* 19.2, 2:246 Hohl).

Besides secular occasions, music was performed in Rome in connection with the cults of foreign divinities. During the ritual ceremonies in honor of Cybele (cf. Catullus *Carmina* 63.19–30; Lucretius *De rerum nat.* 2.618 ff.) melodies of Phrygian origin were executed to the beat of cymbals and kettledrums and to the accompaniment of *elymoi*—auloi of different lengths, one of which ended with a bell curved backward. These same instruments were also employed in the dionysiac rituals, the *Bacchanalia*. The cult of Isis, which gained adherents especially after the conquest of Egypt (31 B.C.), made the Romans acquainted with the melodies and dances of the Nile valley as well as with the sistrum, an instrument made of metal plates that chimed when shaken by the priests (cf. Apuleius *Metamorphoses* 11.4 ff.).[8]

In this diverse and mixed cultural milieu, the spring of Christian song originated in the first and second century. The first believers who constituted the church of Rome were Jews, and we can certainly identify Hebrew psalmody as one of the fundamental elements of the earliest Christian music.[9] But as Christianity spread throughout the empire and penetrated very different cultural and social contexts, liturgical song became enriched with heterogeneous features that helped detach it from the music of the synagogues. The influence of Greco-Roman music doubtless played a role in the birth of Christian song. The oldest Christian hymn we know is in Greek, with Greek musical notation written on the text (*POxy.* 1786 of the third or fourth century).[10] But the ideological conflict between Christians and pagans that led to the violent repression and persecutions, and forced the church underground for almost three centuries, also had an effect on the cult's music. Christian music tended to assume autonomous forms in order to differentiate itself from secular music, which was the target of harsh criticism from the first Christian authors (cf. Ps.-Cipr. *De spect.* 2 ff., 4:811 ff. Migne; Arnob. *Adv. nat.* 2.42, pp. 115–16 Marchesi).

In 313 Constantine granted religious freedom to the Christians, and later Theodosius made Christianity the official religion of the state. Liturgical song began to respond to a new openness toward ever more numerous groups of believers. In order to satisfy the need for choral participation in the ritual, Christian liturgy added to the solo psalmody and to the responsorial song (where the people would answer with a brief final sequence to the melody of the soloist) the antiphonal song, executed by the whole congregation in two semichoruses. These modes of vocal expression constituted the starting point for the subsequent development of musical forms in the Middle Ages. At the fall of the Western Empire, only the music of the church survived the demise of the classical musical tradition and was able to provide a fundamental contribution to the rise of national musical cultures.

After a period of evolution which spanned more than a millennium, the cycle of Greek and Roman musical civilization came to a close. Of ancient music nothing survives. Only literary sources and the theoretical works remain to document the significance of musical phenomena in the ancient world.

Four

Musical Instruments

Stringed Instruments

The description and analysis of the specific features of ancient Greek musical instruments must perforce be based first of all on a few rare archaeological finds. We have examples of lyres in the British Museum and in the Leiden Museum and of auloi in the National Museum of Naples, in the Museum of Cairo, and in the British Museum. But the most abundant and precise information on the subject derives from representations in the figurative arts, both pictorial and plastic, and in particular from a great number of vase paintings, many of which are fairly detailed. Other facts concerning instruments and their use are known to us from literary sources, from Homer to writers of the fifth century A.D. Especially valuable in this respect are the works of lexicographers and scholars. In the fourth book of his *Onomasticon* (chaps. 58–62, 67–77), Pollux (second century) lists a remarkable series of instruments, with occasional brief descriptions and references. The *Deipnosophistai* of Athenaeus (second century), chiefly the fourth and fourteenth books, include substantial discussions of musical instruments. This text is a unique and irreplaceable source of information about the different types of auloi and, above all, about the structural characteristics, the tonal range, and the uses of harps.

The major difficulty one meets in classifying the Greek instruments consists in matching with any certainty, or at least with sufficient plausibility, the names and features mentioned by literary sources with the different types of instruments represented in ancient art. The terms and related descriptions found in the ancient authors often appear to fit more than one pictorial representation of a given class of instrument. We are therefore able to subdivide the instruments only in the broadest organological categories: strings, winds, and percussion. Among stringed instruments, we can distinguish those with strings of equal length (lyres, citharae, etc.), those with strings of different lengths (harps), and those with a single long neck (lutes).

The study of the musical instruments used in ancient Greece is necessarily related to a more general knowledge of the organology of the Eastern Mediterranean countries. We must always remember that the areas of diffusion of individual instruments cross the geographical and linguistic boundaries of the different regions of Greece, especially in the direction of Asia Minor and the East. Moreover, the Greeks themselves in their mythological stories about the origins of such instruments as the auloi tended to attribute them to settings beyond the boundaries of the Greek *oikoumene*. Only the *chelys*, the turtle shell, which represents the most rudimentary form of instrument with strings of equal length, was born in Peloponnesian Kyllene (*Homeric Hymn to Hermes* 39 ff.). It almost seems as though this myth meant to reclaim for the instruments derived from the *chelys*—the lyre and the cithara— some measure of Greek originality and autochthony. As a matter of fact, the presence of different types of lyres and citharae throughout Middle Eastern organology as early as the Sumerian age does not allow us to ascribe to the Greeks the exclusive paternity of such instruments.

According to the myth just mentioned, and probably also in historical reality, the first lyre utilized as its sound box (*echeion*) a turtle shell to which the horns of an animal (*pecheis*) were attached,

Figure 4. Amphora by Eucharides Painter showing Artemis (right) and Apollo (left) playing the lyre, his left hand holding the plektron tied to the lyre by a cord. About 490 B.C.

joined at the top by a crosspiece (*zygon*). The strings were secured to the crosspiece and connected at the other end to the shell by means of a string bar (*chordotonon*) and a bridge (*magas*). The latter was a support for the strings; made of soft wood, the bridge had the function of transmitting to the sound box the vibrations of the strings when they were plucked by the player. The strings themselves were apparently stretched and tuned in very rudimentary fashion. Even though scholars do not agree in interpreting the literary and archaeological information, the strings seem to have been wound around the *zygon* and held fast by means of a piece of hide (*kollops* or *kollabos*) cut from the neck of an animal and spread with sticky grease, so that it would adhere tightly to the wound-up string and hold it in place. It is evident that such a system could give no guarantee that the tuning would be accurate or hold up, especially if one takes into account the poor quality of the strings. These were made of strands of twisted animal gut or sinew, and had unequal thickness and variable elasticity not proportionate to their thickness. We know of particular forms of tuning meant for subdividing the tone in four parts and determining different *chroai,* or tone colors, which required moving the pitch of the inner sounds of the tetrachord by a minimal fraction. But we must assume that these types of tuning, given the precision attributed to them, must have existed only in the theoretical treatises. In practice, a reasonable degree of approximation was probably the most one could aim for, while a perfect tuning would be far out of reach. The unreliability of tuning is probably one of the reasons why the practice of combining together the sound of several instruments (*synaulia*) was never widespread in ancient Greece. The number of strings of the lyre did not remain constant but varied in the course of time, going from a minimum of four to a maximum of eleven or twelve.[1] This change was due to the requirement of increasing the tonal range of the instrument and of subdividing the intervals into even smaller fractions.

The most common stringed instruments in Greece were those with strings of equal length. Within this substantially unitarian type, we can distinguish two subgroups: the instruments in which the arms are structurally distinct from the resounding body, and those in which the arms represent a prolongation of it. To the first belongs the *chelys,* which we have already described and which is most frequently depicted in art. We must also mention an instrument with a small sound box and long, curved arms joined by a short *zygon*—features which imply low volume and, given the length of the strings, a low pitch. This instrument has been identified with the *barbitos,* which was dear to the poets of Lesbos and must have been popular also in Dionysiac settings, as its presence in komos scenes and its association with the *krotala,* or castanets, seem to indicate.[2] It must have been played chiefly indoors, in front of a small audience, such as the guests of a banquet or a thiasos. Vase paintings sometimes represent in addition a different type of lyre, which has a semicircular box with a straight base and curved arms like those of the *barbitos* though much shorter. It has

Figure 5. Oinochoe by Berlin Painter showing barbitos player and boy.
About 490–480 B.C.

been called *Thamyris-kithara* by M. Wegner because it appears in a
representation of the saga of the Thracian singer (Oxford 530; *CVA*
Oxford 2.1, fig. 32, 1).[3] Yet another type of lyre, very similar to the
preceding one, has the sound box in the shape of a prism with
rectangular base. Its arms are of unequal length and rise from the
top side, holding a crosspiece as long as the whole instrument. Its
structure is very similar to that of the Sumerian lyre from Ur
(second millennium B.C.) now in the University Museum in Phila-
delphia: this is a wooden lyre of remarkable size, probably meant
for performances in large halls like the royal palace of Ur, in whose
necropolis it was found.

The lyre was always regarded as the instrument of the free man,
the preeminently "aristocratic" instrument. Boys would learn music on the lyre repeating by ear the melodies played by their
teacher (Plato, *Laws* 7.812b–813a). During banquets the lyre ac-

companied the *skolia*—traditional sympotic songs—or the improvisations of the guests. Those who did not know how to play were considered rustic and uneducated, as happened to Themistocles when he refused the lyre at a symposium (Ion, *FGrHist* 392 F 13). Professional musicians, on the other hand, preferred stringed instruments with a bigger sound box integrally joined to the arms, whose loud volume made them suited to performances in large, open spaces. The most famous of these, the instrument of bards, frequently mentioned in the Homeric poems, is the *phorminx*. This has been identified with an instrument depicted on vases of the Geometric style (the *kanne* of the Dipilon, Tübingen, n. inv. 2657), having a semicircular sound box from which arms extend perpendicular to the end of the diameter of the *echeion*.[4] Normally it has four strings. If in some representations we see three only, we should probably regard it as an error by the painter rather than believe in the existence of an instrument with such a restricted tonal range.

To formulate a hypothesis about the tuning of the four-string instrument is a difficult undertaking. The basic system of Greek musical theory was the tetrachord, with an interval of a fourth (two and a half tones) between the highest and lowest notes; the two inner notes assumed a different position according to the genera—diatonic, enharmonic, and chromatic—and colorings (*chroai*). It has been assumed, therefore, that this represented also the tuning of the oldest four-string instruments. M. L. West bases his recent discussion on an analysis of the notes that appear in all the schemes of the ancient harmoniae as reported by Aristides Quintilianus (*De mus.* 1.9, p. 18, 5 ff. W.-I.), who probably took them from the Damonic tradition (*De mus.* 2.14, p. 80, 29 W.-I.).[5] West takes into account the differences in tone between tonic and atonic syllables in a language with pitch accent such as the Greek, and formulates the hypothesis that the *phorminx* was tuned on the notes mi (*hypate*)—fa (*lichanos*)—la (*mese*)—re (*nete*). He then goes on to propose a musical reading of the first lines of the *Iliad*. It is more probable, however, that the tunings of the stringed instruments of ancient Greece would not always be the same, but rather, would vary according to the nature of the passage to be performed

Figure 6. Amphora showing kithara being played. About 460 B.C.

and the requirements of the performer himself, who no doubt adapted his instrument to match the range of the voice of the singer he had to accompany.

The preeminent concert instrument was the *kithara*, whose resounding body, of considerable size, was shaped like an isosceles trapezium set on its shorter side and narrowing drastically at the base of the short and stumpy arms. It was an instrument for professional musicians (cf. Aristot. *Pol.* 1341a17). If we are right in identifying it with the *asias* mentioned by Pseudo-Plutarch (*De mus.* 6.1133c), it may have been Eastern in origin. According to Pseudo-Plutarch, Cepion, a disciple of Terpander, was the first to build the Asian cithara on the island of Lesbos. It was heavy, with seven strings, and elaborately crafted, with carvings and inlays of ivory and fine woods. In vase paintings it is generally played by men, in some cases by Maenads (*CVA* Br.Mus. 3 He fig. 42 lb = Gr.Brit. 162) and Nike (*CVA* Oxford 3.1 fig. 15, 1 = Gr.Brit. 107), almost never by ordinary women. The cithara acquired greater and greater importance in the Greek musical world as solo performance became progressively more virtuosic and required the use of adequate instruments by professional artists.

In vase paintings of the end of the sixth and of the fifth century B.C., we find an instrument which combines features of the cithara and the *phorminx*. It has a semicircular sound box, similar to that of the *phorminx* but larger; its arms are sturdy and close together and reminiscent of the cithara, even though they appear longer and more slender; it has seven strings, three more than the *phorminx*, and it must have produced a volume greater than the *phorminx* but not as loud as the cithara. In art it appears played almost always by women. We do not know its proper name, but since it represented an upgraded model of the phorminx, it was probably referred to by the same name. Modern scholars have coined for it the term *Wiegen-kithara* on account of the shape of its sound box, which recalls a cradle seen from the front.[6]

Harps were generally played indoors and appear represented almost always in the hands of women. These instruments had little importance in the musical life of the Greeks and were regarded as alien to the Greek musical tradition and imported from foreign cultures. Unlike the lyre and the cithara, they had no role in education. But it is a harp that appears in the oldest extant representation of a stringed instrument in Greek art: a marble statuette of a harpist dating from the second millennium B.C., found at Keros on the island of Thera (now in the Metropolitan Museum of Art; Rogers Fund, 1947, n. 47.100.1). The *polychordia* typical of harps is criticized by Plato (*Rep.* 3.399d), who does not include them among the instruments accepted in his city because they can produce also harmoniae different from the Dorian and the Phrygian, the only ones that imitate the words and modes of those who show valour in war and the gift of persuasion in peace.

Ancient writers apply to this category of instruments a variety of different names: *trigonon, psalterion, sambyke, magadis, pektis, phoinix, spadix, iambyke, nablas, epigoneion, simiakon, lyrophoinikion, pariambos, pelex.* We find several, although not as many, different types of harp represented in pictorial and plastic art beginning from the middle of the fifth century B.C. R. Herbig classifies them on the basis of four different types.[7] The first has an upper sound box curved slightly forward and connected at an acute angle to a narrow soundbox base. The strings are stretched between the soundbox and the base. The second has an apparently fusiform resounding body, with a framework made of five sticks. In the third the frame is triangular, and each of its components should serve as sound box. The fourth and most common type has an upper resounding body curved forward to a pronounced degree, and a base made of two parallel elements; the strings are attached to the upper element by means of the *kollaboi* or *kollopes*. The third side of the harp can either be open or closed by a straight piece which connects the resounding body to the base and which can also be in the shape of a stylized bird, probably in imitation of Egyptian or Middle Eastern models.

An ancient name may be attributed with any degree of certainty only to the harps of the second group—the "fusiform harps," as R. Herbig defines them—which were probably called *magadides*. The correct interpretation of a passage of Telestes (fr. 808 P.), where the *magadis* is described as a "five-stick instrument," finds exact correspondence in the frame of the fusiform harp, which is constructed, again, of five sticks. Anacreon attributes twenty strings to the *magadis* (fr. 96 Gent.), the same number of strings as the fusiform harp represented on a vase in the Metropolitan Museum of New York (Rogers Fund, 1907, 07.286.35a–b). Also the different slant of the upper arm with respect to the base, a slant which increases in the part where the longest strings are stretched, makes sense in an instrument like the *magadis*, where one half of the strings must correspond to the other half at the interval of an octave.[8]

Identification of other harp types with the instruments mentioned by Athenaeus and Pollux appears highly problematic and uncertain because the ancient authors have given us little information about the shape of the instruments. Only with respect to the *sambyke* can we risk a hypothesis. The same word was used for a floating siege machine described by Polybius (8.4.2), which in its form and structure recalls the musical instrument. The machine was constructed of two ships tied side by side: on the ships was a ladder built so that it could be lowered forward toward the prow by means of pulleys attached to the masts, and long enough to reach beyond the rostra once it was lowered. The ladder was protected at the top and sides and, at the end, it held a platform on which four men could fight facing the enemy. The rowers would move the machine near the walls of the city, and the ladder would then be lowered so that the platform rested on the walls and the besiegers could get on top of the walls and fight level with the defenders. This device looked very much like a harp frame constructed on a heavy base, which served as sound box, with a rather solid arm at a considerable slant and an end piece—corresponding to the platform at the end of the ladder—parallel to the base and reaching beyond the base itself. A harp represented on a *pelike* in the National Museum of Naples (n. inv. 3231), belonging to the fourth type, appears to have this shape.[9] Such an identification, however, does not agree with the testimony of Euphorion in Athenaeus (14.633 ff.) that the *sambyke* used by the Parthians and the Troglodites had only four strings. This statement implicitly excludes the possibility that this *sambyke* was a harp, since the latter is by definition a *polychordos* instrument. It is possible that Euphorion applied the term *sambyke* to another type of cordo-

Figure 7. Lebes gamikos by Washing Painter showing wedding preparations, woman seated playing trignon harp. About 430–420 B.C.

phone which had some features in common with the harp in question. In any case, the *sambyke* must have been a small instrument with short strings, and this would account for its high pitch and effeminate sound (Arist. Quint. *De mus.* 2.16, p. 85, 10 ff., W.-I.).

As to the other names of harps, *trigonon*, "triangular harp," possibly indicates instruments such as those of Herbig's third type (e.g., the *hydria* of the Br.Mus. E228, Cat. of Vases 3.180s, fig. 9, described and reproduced by Herbig, 177–78). *Psalterion* indicates "any instrument to be played without a plectrum, to be plucked with the fingers" (*psallein*). The word occurs eight times in the Septuagint Bible, where it renders the Hebrew *nevel*, which is also translated fourteen times by *nabla*. All three terms seem to indicate a triangular harp, probably to be identified with some instrument of the third type in Herbig's classification. This is only a hypothesis, however. The names *iambyke, klepsiambos,* and *pariambos* refer to the type of execution for which the instruments were employed and cannot provide any information on their shape and character. The *pektis* was a harp that must have had the same features as the *magadis*: Aristoxenus (fr. 98 Wehrli) and Menaechmus of Sicyon (*FGrHist.* 131 F 4) maintain that they were the same instrument. But no testimony about the shape of this instrument is extant. Of the *epigoneion* and the *simiakon* we know the number of the strings—forty and thirty-five, respectively (Pollux *Onomasticon* 4.60). C. Sachs formulates the hypothesis that the *epigoneion* was so called because one would play it holding it on the knees, like a modern zither.[10] On the question of the names of harps there was no doubt some confusion even among ancient scholars. Euphorion (Athenaeus 14.635 ff.) states in his work *On the Isthmian Games* that many-string instruments—i.e., harps—differ from one another in name only. It is evident that already in the third century B.C. it was no longer possible to connect a certain name to a specific sort of instrument.

Finally, mention should be made of the *tripous* of Pythagoras of Zacynthus (mid-fifth century B.C.). According to a description of Artemon (Athen. 14.637b), it consisted of a revolving stand shaped like a tripod with a resounding body on top, in the place of the lebes, and three sets of strings on the three sides, each tuned to a different harmonia—Dorian, Phrygian, and Lydian. The *tripous,* which according to Artemon never became very popular, allowed its inventor to play in the three harmoniae without changing instruments or tuning.

After the middle of the fourth century a type of lute called *pandoura* (or *pandouron*) appeared in Greece. It had a small, pear-shaped sound box and a long neck on which three strings were stretched (Poll. *Onom.* 4.60). It was devised by the Assyrians (Pollux *loc. cit.*) and by the Troglodites, a people inhabiting the area south of Lydia (Athen. 4.183 f.; Herodotus 4.183). Perhaps the *skindapsos,* a four-string instrument, was also a lute.[11]

Wind Instruments

Among wind instruments, the most common was certainly the double aulos, widespread throughout Greece. In the earliest times each of the two pipes (*bombyx*) had four borings (*trypemata*) until Diodorus of Thebes increased their number (Poll. *Onom.* 4.80). Pronomus, also of Thebes, a teacher of Alcibiades (Athen. 4.184d) was the first to succeed in playing in all the harmoniae on the same instrument (Paus. 9.12.6; Athen. 14.631e). He must therefore have

Figure 8. Cup of Epictetus showing aulos player using a phorbeia and dancer playing krotala. About 500 B.C. British Museum E38.

had to increase further the number of holes and, consequently, to have equipped the instrument with keys—rings of metal for closing each hole—which would allow the aulete to vary the tuning as the performance demanded. The aulos had reeds (*glottai*) inserted in a narrowing (*zeugos*) which connected the mouthpiece to two bulges (*holmoi*) in the pipe; between these and the pipe there was another narrowing (*hypholmion*). It must therefore be a mistake to render *aulos* as "flute," as is normally done: the modern instrument most similar to the ancient aulos is the oboe. Auletes would often wear a *phorbeia* (Lat. *capistrum*), a sort of leather halter with two holes into which the two mouthpieces were inserted. It probably served to compress the cheeks in order to facilitate blowing into the pipes.

Playing the aulos required considerable professional ability. The best auletes were in great demand in Athens for preparing and accompanying dithyrambic, tragic, and comic choruses. But for all that these musicians were appreciated and sought after, the aulos was never considered an instrument suitable to the education of free men. It is true that not infrequently even prominent people would receive instruction from distinguished masters: Alcibiades was taught the rudiments of aulos playing by Pronomus of Thebes (Athen. 4.184d), and Epaminondas by Olympiodorus and Ortagoras (Athen. 4.184e). But the aulos was mainly an instrument for professionals, and in the scale of social values the Greeks never held in high regard anyone who exercised a professional activity, even at a high level: they still considered the professional a *banausos* (Aristot. *Pol.* 8.1340b20 ff.). This notion also explains the contrast between the aulos and the lyre in favor of the latter, a contrast which inspired several mythological tales. The satyr aulete Marsyas won the music contest with Apollo but ended up flayed alive by his divine competitor (Diod. Sic. 3.59.2–5). In the dithyramb *Marsyas*, Melanippides (fr. 758 P) refers to the myth of the origin of aulos playing and reports that when Athena noticed that blowing into the pipes deformed her cheeks, she cast away the instrument she had herself created; the Phrygian Marsyas picked it up and played it with great skill. This story is countered by another dithyrambic poet, Telestes (fr. 805 P), who argues that Athena could not have thrown away the auloi for that reason, because a virgin goddess would not have paid so much attention to her beauty; rather, Athena entrusted the instrument to Dionysus, to whom she also taught the technique of aulos playing.

Telestes defended the aulos as an instrument connected with the Dionysiac tradition of the dithyramb. Melanippides, on the other hand, was an innovator who included in the dithyramb soloistic parts, probably accompanied by the stringed instrument; his narrative therefore meant to emphasize the subordination of the Dionysiac aulos to the Apollinean cithara. Melanippides was criticized by Democritus of Chios (Aristot. *Rhet.* 3.1409b17) for having excessively expanded the *anabolai,* soloistic introductions that had evidently come to occupy disproportionate space with respect to the choral singing.

The contrast between lyre and aulos is further underlined by the fact that the whole Greek tradition agrees in attributing to the latter a foreign origin, Phrygian or in any case Eastern, while the lyre is considered an autochthonous and preeminently Hellenic instrument. Plato does not accept the aulos among the instruments admitted in his state on account of its *polychordia*. It can produce too great a number of different sounds and can therefore play in all the harmoniae (*Rep.* 3.399d). Evidently Plato refers to the instrument as it was enhanced and modified by the innovations of Pronomus of Thebes. But the aulos would have met with Plato's disapproval simply because of the psychagogic and orgiastic nature of its sound, which was not conducive to equilibrium and calm, but rather, disturbed the listener and excited the irrational part of the soul.

It appears clear from vase paintings that in each pair of auloi the pipes were of equal length, with the holes in the same position. It is therefore difficult to establish the respective functions of the two instruments in the musical performance. The first might have played the melody, while the other played the accompaniment with sustained notes or with simple variations; or they may have played alternatively, rather than simultaneously, one on the lower and the other on the higher pitch according to the texture of the musical composition. No information is easily available that might help us determine on which notes and according to which intervals the auloi were tuned. Research on the pipes and on the respective holes of the extant auloi has yielded inconsistent results with regard to the tunings of the instruments and the pitch of the intervals, which do not appear to coincide with those described in the theoretical treatises for the different *tonoi* or scales.[12] In his *Harmonic Elements* (2.37), Aristoxenus remarks significantly on the considerable differences that exist between the succession of the *tonoi* in the system of the *Harmonikoi* (i.e., of the theorists) on the one hand, and in the system adopted by the makers of auloi on the other. According to the first system, for example, the interval between the first note of a Hypophrygian tone and the first note of the Hypodorian is one tone, while according to the other system the interval is three *dieseis* (¾ tone). We are dealing with a diverse and multiform musical landscape, where each type of instrument, or even each individual instrument, has its special tuning. Such a musical system is so different from our own, based entirely on the uniformity of tunings, that it often appears unimaginable and incomprehensible.

The auloi were distinguished according to the pitch of the sound they produced. The low-pitched auloi—the *teleioi* and the *hyperteleioi*—accompanied songs of male choruses; the *kitharis-terioi* were tuned for joining the sound of the cithara in the *syn-aulia;* the *parthenioi* and the *paidikoi* played at a higher octave in order to suit the pitch of choruses of women and boys (Poll. *Onom.* 4.8; Aristox. fr. 101 Wehrli = Athen. 14.634e). There were also auloi pitched and tuned especially for accompanying particular forms of choral song. The *aulema gamelion,* a wedding song, was played by two auloi at the mutual interval of an octave, the lower aulos for the bridegroom, the higher for the bride. The *auloi paroinioi,* which were small and high-pitched, were played at symposia; the *spondeiakoi,* "of libations," accompanied hymns; the *Pythikoi* accompanied paeans as well as playing the Pythian nomos (see above, p. 16); the *auloi chorikoi* accompanied dithyrambs; the *paratretoi,* high-pitched auloi "with holes on the side" accompanied the *threnoi.* The ecstatic and perturbing character of the *bombykes* made them suitable to orgiastic ceremonies, while the *embaterioi* and the *daktyloi* were the auloi appropriate to *prosodia* and *hyporchemata* (Poll. *Onom.* 4.80–82).

All these types of auloi differed only in the position of the holes and, consequently, in the tuning. In shape and structure they were all alike. This fact can to some extent also explain the remark with which Pollux (*Onom.* 4.82) concludes his list, that "some people say that these are not types (*eide*) of auloi, but of melodies." As a matter of fact, to each genre of song or of musical piece corresponded a special tuning of the instruments and therefore a special type of aulos.

Other auloi, also mentioned and described by Pollux (*Onom.* 4.74–77), must have differed in shape as well. They were mostly single rather than double, and were recently imported from foreign countries. The *aulos plagios,* "transverse" like our modern flute, was made out of lotus and came from Lydia, as did the *hippophorbos,* a high-pitched instrument used by nomadic horse breeders. The *monaulos* was of Egyptian origin and was used for wedding songs. Another *monaulos,* from Caria and Phrygia, was employed to accompany funerary lamentations. The same should be said for the *ghingras,* a small Phoenician instrument connected with the cult of Adonis and Cybele. A small curved instrument appears in a Corybantic group represented in a famous Pompeian mosaic of Dioscourides (see Figure 9); here the reference to a scene from Menander's *Theophoroumene* and certain unusual structural features of the instrument suggest that the latter should be identified with the *ghingras.*[13]

Among the Scyths, the Androphagi, the Melanchlaeni, and the Arimaspeans used to build wind instruments out of eagle and vulture bones. Other types of aulos are the *polyphthongoi,* whose invention was traditionally attributed to Osiris; the *mesokopoi,* "of middle thickness"; the *pyknoi;* the *diopoi,* "with two holes"; the *hemiopoi,* "with three holes"; the *hypopteroi,* "winged" (?); and the *idouthoi.* There was also a type of aulos called *Athena* because Nicopheles, a Theban aulete, had used it for the nomos of Athena. Finally, the *elymos* was a type of aulos with very peculiar features. It had pipes of different lengths: the longest ended with a bell curved backwards, while the shorter must have been tuned to high pitches. It was an instrument of Phrygian origin, used especially in the rituals of the cult of Cybele.

Other aerophones entirely different in structure from the aulos were also widespread in the ancient world. First of all, the *syrinx* consisted in a series of pipes of decreasing pitch bound together; the Greeks attributed its invention to Pan. It had no importance whatsoever in their musical life and was rather universally considered as an instrument suitable at most for easing the toil of shepherds. Perhaps because of its irrelevance on the paideutic and cultural levels, Plato accepts the *syrinx* in his state as useful in the country to the herdsmen (*Rep.* 3.399d).

The *syrinx* deserves mention too because it represented the starting point for building the only musical instrument of antiquity with mechanical works, the *hydraulis* or *Tyrrenos aulos* (cf. Poll. *Onom.* 4.70). It consisted of an upside-down *syrinx* into whose pipes air was fed from below by means of a mechanism that utilized water pressure. Its invention is attributed to Ctesibius, a barber from Alexandria of the third century B.C. (Athen. 4.176b). In addition to the descriptions in the *Pneumatika* of Heron (1.42) and in the *De architectura* of Vitruvius (10.8), we have numerous pictorial and plastic representations, a few fragments of pipes found at Pompeii, and the remains of a small instrument dating from A.D. 228 preserved in the museum at Aquincum near Budapest. The *hydraulis* enjoyed some popularity during the late Hellenistic and Roman age, in part because the piercing sonority of the larger and more sophisticated instruments was eminently suitable to the spacious places where performances were held in that period (amphitheaters, circuses, arenas), and in part because their tuning permitted the execution of music in different tonalities (*tropos Hyperlydios, Hyperiastios, Lydios, Phrygos, Hypolydios, Hypophrygios,* according to *Anon.Bell.* 2.28, p. 8, 6 Najock). This feature made the *hydraulis* particularly suited to producing music of the imitative and virtuosic sort, free from harmonic restrictions and from any obligation of tonal coherence.

Kerata (horns) and *salpinges* (trumpets) were normally used for the practical purpose of military communication rather than for musical performances, even though they were sometimes used in musical events, especially in Roman times. *Kerata* were small and made of cow horns.[14] The *salpinges,* of Etruscan origin, were straight trumpets of considerable length: an ivory exemplar preserved in the Boston Museum of Fine Arts measures 1.57 meters. They were generally made of bronze, with a fairly wide bell and a cup-shaped mouthpiece similar to that of modern brass instruments. *Kochloi,* derived from large shells, were instruments for naval signaling, and are mentioned in Euripides (*Iph. Taur.* 303).

In Roman times, to the brass *salpinx* (Lat. *tuba*) other types of metal military trumpets were added. The *lituus,* the instrument

Figure 9. Mosaic by Dioscourides of Samos showing musicians in a scene from New Comedy. Augustan period. Naples, National Museum 9985.

used by the cavalry, had a high-pitched sound, a straight and slender tube, and a bell that bent upwards. The *cornu* had tubing three meters long, bent in the shape of a circle, with a wooden crosspiece at the diameter which allowed it to rest on the player's shoulders; the bell was conic, pointing forward. The *bucina* was shaped like a bull's horn. These instruments were sometimes used in concerts with large choral groups (see above, p. 53).

Finally, the aerophones also included the *rhombos,* which consisted of a stick or a tablet attached to a string and whirled overhead. The sound it produced when rotated at a relatively slow speed resembled the lowing of a cow (cf. Eur. *Hel.* 1362; see also Diogenes Athen. F 1.3, *TrGF* 1, p. 185 Snell).

Percussion Instruments

Among the Greeks, unlike other ancient peoples, percussion instruments were never widespread nor particularly important. Their use was generally restricted to the rituals of the cults of Dionysus and Cybele, and were always perceived as exotic instruments not connected with the most ancient and genuine traditions of the Greeks. *Tympana* were small drums to be struck with the hand, very similar to the tambourines used in modern folk dances. They did not, however, have bells, and were equipped with handles. A *tympanon* of considerable size held by a dancer-musician is represented in the mosaic of Dioscourides of the National Museum of Naples.[15] The *krotala* consisted of two pieces of wood or metal connected on one side by a hinge which were clapped together with the fingers of one hand, like modern castanets.[16] Another percussion instrument represented in the Pompeian mosaic of Dioscourides are the *kymbala*, or *krembala*, two metal plates, one for each hand, struck together like modern cymbals. *Kymbala* appear only rarely in vase paintings, but we have a few exemplars, now preserved in the museums of Berlin, Athens, London, and Heidelberg. Among percussion instruments we also know of the *kroupalon* (Soph. fr. 44), equivalent to the Roman *scabellum*, consisting of a shoe with double wooden sole, which the aulete would strike on the ground to beat time for the chorus.

Some Apulian and Campanian vases bear the representation of a sort of small ladder which seems to be a musical instrument analogous to the modern xylophone. It has been termed "Apulian sistrum."[17]

Five

Music Theory

A systematic study of the fundamental theoretical principles of ancient Greek music began, as far as we know, at the end of the sixth century B.C. in Athens and Croton, in Southern Italy, by two figures of considerable prominence in the history of Greek culture, Lasus of Hermione and Pythagoras of Samos. As I have already mentioned, Lasus was the first to use the term *harmonia* in a musical sense, increased the number of notes that could be executed on the cithara, and defined the size of intervals in mathematical terms. Pythagoras experimentally proved the existence of defined numerical ratios between consonant sounds at the interval of the fourth, the fifth, and the octave (Nicom. *Ench.* 6, pp. 245 ff. Jan). The same discovery was attributed by Theon of Smyrna to Lasus and to the Pythagorean Hippasus of Metapontum (*Vors.* 1, p. 110, 3 ff. Diels-Kranz).[1]

Two fundamentally different approaches seem to characterize the doctrine of Lasus on the one hand and that of Pythagoras and the Pythagoreans on the other. Lasus bases his musical research on his personal musical practice and on observations derived from listening to the songs of the musical repertory of the Greeks. Pythagoras and his followers, on the other hand, neglect the contemporary musical reality and instead confront problems of acoustic measurement with the help of scientific instruments, such as the monochord, vases filled with water at set levels, and metallic discs of different weights. These measurements, of course, refer to the pitches of sounds in relation to other sounds, and are not absolute. Ancient scholars did not discover with certainty that mechanical vibrations are the phenomena that produce sounds, much less discover an instrument for measuring their frequency. Thus, the ancients were never able to establish a basic sound that would serve as a reference point for all other sounds, such as the A of 440 Hz for our music. For this reason their musical theories were never based on sounds in absolute terms, but on intervals— that is, on relative pitch differences among sounds.

Lasus, then, was the first to identify and examine the different *harmoniai*, namely the tunings (the original meaning of the term in music) which were required to play the *nomoi*, the traditional songs of the different parts of Greece. The fragment quoted earlier (*PMG* fr. 702; see above, p. 26)—"I sing of Demeter and of Kore, wife of Klymenos, intoning the sweet hymn on the low-roaring Aeolian harmonia"—is revealing in this respect, since it specifies that the Aeolian harmonia belonged in the range of low-pitched sounds. Damon, a few decades after Lasus, dealt with the harmoniae, too (as we have seen). He argued that in a well-ordered state it was proper to admit in the education of the young only some of the harmoniae, such as the Dorian and the Phrygian, and a few rhythms. The ancient sources do not, however, give us the criteria for defining exactly what musical characteristics, and especially what pitches and succession of intervals, Damon assigned to individual harmoniae.

This is also true of the evidence provided by Plato and Aristotle. Both of them, following Damon, dealt with the ethical character of each harmonia and their pedagogical and psychagogical effects, but no passage in their works specifically mentions the distinctive features of the various harmoniae with regard to the pitch of the voice, the succession of the intervals, and the tuning of the accompanying instruments.[2] Only Aristides Quintilianus (*De mus.* 9, p. 18, 5 ff. Winnington-Ingram), with reference to Plato's *Republic*

(3.399a), has recorded the successions of intervals and the diagrams of the six harmoniae which Plato himself considers in the passage in question. If we transcribe the diagrams into modern notation according to the correspondences that are conventionally accepted, we obtain the following sequences (the enharmonic *diesis,* equivalent to the raising of a quarter-tone is indicated by ‡):

Lydian (*Lydisti*): mi‡, fa, la, ti, ti‡, do₁, mi₁, mi₁‡

Dorian (*Doristi*): sol, la, la‡, la ♯, re, mi₁, mi₁‡, fa₁, la₁

Phrygian (*Phrygisti*): sol, la, la‡, la ♯, re₁, mi₁, mi₁‡, fa₁, sol₁

Ionian (*Iasti*): mi, mi‡, fa, la, do₁, re₁

Mixolydian (*Mixolydisti*): mi, mi‡, fa, sol, la, la‡, la ♯, mi₁

Syntolydian (*Syntonolydisti*): mi, mi‡, fa, la, do₁

As one can see, the harmoniae mentioned by Plato and described by Aristides Quintilianus do not include the low-pitched Aeolian of Lasus's fragment. Also missing are three other harmoniae which are quoted elsewhere by Greek authors: the *Lokristi,* the *Hypodoristi,* and the *Hypophrygisti.* The first had supposedly been employed in ancient times by Xenocritus of Locris (*Schol.* Pind. *Ol.* 10.17k; 10.18b) and was still in use at the time of Pindar and Simonides, though later set aside (Athen. 14.625e) and assimilated to the *Hypodoristi* (Cleon. *Isag.* 9, p. 198, 13 Jan); the latter was in turn only a late name for the Aeolian, and was used in the non-choral parts of tragedy on account of its grand and stately character (Ps.-Aristot. *Probl.* 19.48). The *Hypophrygisti* is supposed to have been used in the same solo parts on account of its essentially practical *ethos* (Ps.-Aristot. *loc. cit.*): they were both particularly suited to musical compositions of the mimetic type (Ps.-Aristot. *Probl.* 19.30).

With regard to the scales described by Aristides, we notice that they include different numbers of sounds: the Dorian and Phrygian have nine, the Lydian and Mixolydian eight, the Ionic six, and the Syntonolydian five. At the same time, the differences in pitch among the various harmoniae are minimal: the difference between the Dorian and the Phrygian harmoniae, for example, appears to consist only in the final notes, a *la*₁ for the Dorian and a *sol*₁ for the Phrygian; the other four sequences all begin with the same note, the *mi*. Both these features are surprising and lead us to believe that either the interval succession specified by Aristides or, more probably, the notes he indicates in his diagrams, may not correspond to the reality of the ancient harmoniae. And yet the presence of the enharmonic *dieseis* in all six sequences suggests an ancient source for the evidence which Aristides provides, since the enharmonic genus, the most ancient and solemn of all, fell out of use before the fourth century B.C. (cf. Aristox. *Harm.* 1.23, p. 29, 14 Da Rios; Ps.-Plut. *De mus.* 38.1145a–c).³ This source may go back to Damonian times because Aristides Quintilianus could still draw, directly or indirectly, from the doctrine of Damon (*De mus.* 2.14, p. 80, 23 ff. W.-I.).

It is nevertheless strange that the Lydian harmonia should be given a tonal range lower by one-third in relation to the Dorian and the Phrygian. According to Pseudo-Plutarch (*De mus.* 15.1136c), Plato excluded it from his educational curriculum precisely on account of its high pitch, characteristic of lamentations. We should note, however, that in the *Republic* (3.398e) Plato describes the Lydian as a soft and relaxed harmonia, suitable to banquets, but makes no mention of its acuteness. We do not know from which source Pseudo-Plutarch derives his remark. In all likelihood the information which Aristides Quintilianus provides on the succession of intervals is reliable, but should be referred to different pitches than those marked on the diagram. Aristides Quintilianus himself (*De mus.* 1.12, p. 30, 1 ff. W.-I.) distinguishes three *tropoi,* or modes, of melodic composition, of which the "nomic" is the most acute, the "dithyrambic" is of middle pitch, and the "tragic" is low. Since the harmoniae characteristic of tragedy were the Mixolydian and the Dorian (Aristox. fr. 81 Wehrli = Ps.-Plut. *De mus.* 16.1136d), we must assume that their tonal range verged on the low notes, while the Phrygian harmonia, which was typical of the dithyramb (Aristot. *Pol.* 8.1342b7), must have been tuned on slightly higher sounds. As Pseudo-Plutarch mentions the discovery of the enharmonic genus by Olympus (*De mus.* 19.1137b ff.; see above, p. 26), he records the succession of the intervals of the *spondeion* (½ tone, 2 tones, 1 tone, ½ tone). The *spondeion* was the style of libations, in which the subdivision of the *pyknon*— i.e., the joining of the two smallest intervals in the enharmonic and chromatic genera—into two quarter-tone intervals, which was characteristic of the enharmonic, had not yet occurred. Also in this case the scale (mi, fa, la, ti, do$_1$) is of only five notes on four tones. It does not even cover the spectrum of an octave, five tones and two semitones.

A discussion of the harmoniae must include an analysis of the different tetrachord types. This succession of four consecutive notes represented the foundation of all the more complete systems of sounds which were elaborated by theorists from Aristoxenus onward. Even though we have no evidence that Lasus and Damon addressed themselves to the problem of defining the tetrachord, one must consider that Lasus felt the need to modify the tuning of the cithara by introducing ever smaller intervals. His purpose was clearly to enable the stringed instrument to execute melodies of the enharmonic genus with the two inner notes of the tetrachord, the *parhypate* and the *lichanos,* at a distance of a quarter tone and a semitone, respectively, from the lowest note, the *hypate* (see above, p. 26). We should also remember that a speech on music by an anonymous rhetor, probably of the fourth century B.C. (*PHibeh* 1.13, reproduced in Sources, below) contests the opinion that the genera of the tetrachord (diatonic, enharmonic, and chromatic) would be able to affect the *ethos* of the listeners and of all of those who employ them in their music. This argument represents additional evidence that the genera were the object of attention in the fourth century and that scholars had already been discussing and defining them for some time.

For us, however, the first theoretical treatment of the subject is that contained in the *Harmonic Elements* of Aristoxenus. For the author, ear, intellect, and memory play a major role in the understanding of musical phenomena and have greater importance than the mathematical calculation of ratios between sounds and the measurement of intervals (*Harm.* 2.38, p. 48, 27 Da Rios).[4] On the strength of this methodological assumption, Aristoxenus considered all the positions that the two inner notes of the tetrachord can occupy within a space reserved to each of them, and he reached the conclusion that the possibilities are infinite. *Parhypate* and *lichanos*, each within its own range, can position themselves at any distance from *hypate* and *mese*, the "fixed" notes of the tetrachord, which stand at a mutual interval of a fourth (two tones and one semitone). Aristoxenus then outlines the three genera of the tetrachord—the enharmonic, the diatonic, and the chromatic—in order to define the ranges within which *parhypate* and *lichanos*, respectively, can be placed; for the last two genera, he also specified the *chroai*, the main nuances or colors, by indicating the measure of the intervals between the four notes:

enharmonic genus: ¼ tone, ¼ tone, 2 tones

chromatic genus *malakon:* ⅓ tone, ⅓ tone, 1⅚ tone

chromatic genus *hemiolion:* ⅜ tone, ⅜ tone, 1¾ tone

chromatic genus *toniaion* or *syntonon:* ½ tone, ½ tone, 1½ tone

diatonic genus *malakon:* ½ tone, ¾ tone, 5/4 tone

diatonic genus *toniaion:* ½ tone, 1 tone, 1 tone

The subdivision of the tetrachord proposed by Aristoxenus is clearly the result of an empirical evaluation of interval size. He makes a first subdivision of the 2 ½ tones of the fourth according to the intervals of the enharmonic genus and of the chromatic and diatonic genera *toniaia* or *syntona;* he then approximates the intervals which specify the *chroai* or nuances, assigning well-defined values to differences in pitch which in musical practice must have been very difficult to quantify.

Other theorists confronted the problem of the subdivision of the tetrachord intervals according to the genera from another avenue, through a purely mathematical process. Pythagoras is said to have been the first to assign a numerical value to each of the four fixed notes of the octave: 12 to *hypate* (mi), 9 to *mese* (la), 8 to *paramese* (ti), 6 to *nete* (mi_1).[5] In this way the octave interval was defined by the double ratio 12 : 6 (= 2 : 1), the interval of a fourth by the epitritic ratio 12 : 9 or 8 : 6 (= 4 : 3), the interval of a fifth by the hemiolian ratio 12 : 8 or 9 : 6 (= 3 : 2), and the interval of a tone by the ratio 9:8 (cf. Nicom. *Ench.* 6, p. 245.19 Jan). In order to establish these values, Pythagoras used the monochord, or *kanon*, simple or double (Theon. 12, p. 59 Hiller), for measuring the length of the strings that produced notes consonant to the octave, the fifth, and the fourth.

Philolaus of Tarentum divided the octave into five tones and two *dieseis* or semitones (cf. Nicom. *Ench.* 9, p. 253.1 Jan), and assigned to the four strings of the tetrachord the following numeric values: 192 to *mese*, 216 to *lichanos*, 243 to *parhypate*, 256 to *hypate*. These values result from arithmetical operations that derive from the Pythagorean ratios 4:3 for the fourth and 9:8 for the tone. If from the ratio of the fourth one subtracts the sum of the ratios of the two tones

$$9/8 \cdot 9/8 = 81/64; \; 4/3 \div 81/64 = 4/3 \cdot 64/81 = 256/243,$$

one obtains the ratio pertaining to the semitone, defined by the numbers 243 and 256. According to the ratio 9:8, the value corresponding to 243, at the distance of a tone, is 216 (9:8 = $243:x; \; x = \dfrac{243 \cdot 8}{9} = 216$), and to the latter, always at the distance of a tone, the value is 192 (9:8 = $216:x; \; x = \dfrac{216 \cdot 8}{9}$ = 192).

With these values established, the size of the first interval of a tone may be represented by the difference between 216 and 192, that is 24; the size of the second interval, also of a tone, by the difference between 243 and 216, that is 27; the size of the third interval, of a semitone, by the difference between 256 and 243, that is 13. One notices with surprise that the sizes of the two tones are not equal, and that the size of the semitone does not correspond to half of the size of each of the two tones. According to Boethius (*De mus.* 3.8), Philolaus distinguished the greater semitone (or *apotome*), defined by the number 14, from the lesser semitone (or *leimma*), defined by the number 13, which added to 14 gives 27, precisely the size of the major tone.

Other calculations of the sizes of intervals are attributed to Archytas of Tarentum (first half of the fourth century B.C.). Archytas defines the intervals of the enharmonic genus (2 tones, ¼ tone, ¼ tone, according to the ratios $\frac{5}{4}$, $\frac{36}{35}$, $\frac{28}{27}$), those of the chromatic genus (1 ½, ½ tone, ½ tone, according to the ratios $\frac{32}{27}$, $\frac{243}{224}$, $\frac{28}{27}$), and those of the diatonic genus (1 tone, 1 tone, ½ tone, according to the ratios $\frac{9}{8}$, $\frac{8}{7}$, $\frac{28}{27}$). The sum of the ratios pertaining to each genus always yields the result $\frac{4}{3}$, the ratio of the fourth (Ptol. *Harm.* 1.13, p. 13 Düring).

Euclid (fourth to third century B.C.) in his *Sectio Canonis* (pp. 148–66 Jan), after an introduction in which he comes very close to formulating the concept of vibration as the phenomenon that generates sound, announces and demonstrates a series of theorems on the ratios between sounds of different pitch and between the lengths of the strings that produce them, as measured with the monochord (*kanon*). His work thus establishes the logical basis of all possible mathematical operations concerning intervals and their ratios.

Claudius Ptolemy (second century) devotes the first book of his *Harmonica* to the study of consonant intervals and to the critical analysis of both the measurements of the inner intervals of the tetrachord and of the definitions of their ratios by Aristoxenus and Archytas. He finally proposes his own ratios, which concern the three genera as well as their respective *chroai* (*Harm.* 7.15, p. 33 ff. Düring). These are, for the enharmonic, $\frac{5}{4}$, $\frac{24}{23}$, and $\frac{46}{45}$; for the chromatic *malakon*, $\frac{6}{5}$, $\frac{15}{14}$, $\frac{28}{27}$; for the chromatic *syntonon*, $\frac{7}{6}$, $\frac{12}{11}$, $\frac{22}{21}$; for the diatonic *toniaion*, $\frac{9}{8}$, $\frac{8}{7}$, $\frac{28}{27}$; finally, for the diatonic *syntonon*, $\frac{10}{9}$, $\frac{9}{8}$, and $\frac{16}{15}$. Also, his measurements take into account the data established by the Pythagoreans and demonstrated by Euclid: if one considers as the size of the interval of one tone the ratio between a fourth and a fifth ($\frac{3}{2}:\frac{4}{3} = \frac{9}{8}$), it follows that the octave (2:1) is smaller by six tones; the semitones cannot be exactly half the tone because $\frac{9}{8}$ is not divisible by two, and neither are the fourth and fifth exactly two and a half tones and three and a half tones.

All that I have said concerning the inner intervals of the tetrachord clearly confirms my initial statement that theoretical research on Greek music always developed on two distinct levels. It was based, on the one hand, on the data derived from listening to musical performances, and on the other, on the numerical results of experimental acoustic-mathematical inquiries. The nineteenth book of the pseudo-Aristotelian *Problems* belongs to the first group. It is a sometimes unique, always important source of information and observation concerning the different aspects of vocal and instrumental practice. In particular, the numerous "problems" dealing with the difficulties of the tuning of songs, of the accompaniment at an interval of an octave, a fourth, or a fifth, or of the particular values of notes, the *mese* (these are *Probl.* 20 and 36, which have led some scholars to regard the *mese* as the proper tonic note), provide irreplaceable evidence on the practice of ancient vocal music. *Problems* 30 and 48, which deal with the Hypodorian and Hypophyrgian harmoniae used in tragic monodies but not in choral songs, are among the latest testimonies we have about the character of the harmoniae. In the work of Aristoxenus, for example, this aspect finds no mention, and even the term *harmonia* itself invariably refers exclusively to the enharmonic genus. Only in one passage (*Harm.* 2.36, p. 46, 10 Da Rios)—where the text happens also to be uncertain—does the term seem to designate the tuning of an instrument and the musical scale.

Aristoxenus was no doubt the first ancient scholar, or one of the first, to concern himself with systems larger than the tetrachord. In a passage of his *Harmonic Elements* (1.6, p. 10, 13 Da Rios) we find for the first time mention of the *systema teleion,* the "perfect system," even though a specific discussion of the subject is nowhere included in the work. The definition of *systema* and the description of systems starting from the smallest, the tetrachord, occur in the handbooks of Aristides Quintilianus (*De mus.* 1.18, p. 13, 4 W.-I.), Cleonides (*Isag.* 1, p. 180, 2 Jan; 8, p. 193, 3 Jan), Nicomachus (*Ench.* 12, p. 261, 19 Jan), Baccheius (*Isag.* 1.6, p. 292, 18 Jan; 1.26 ff., p. 298, 19 Jan), Gaudentius (*Isag.* 4, p. 330, 21 Jan; 18, p. 345, 13 Jan), Anon. Bellermann (3.51, p. 15, 4 Najock). The concordances in the definitions and descriptions suggest that all these passages go back to a single Aristoxenian source. For the ancient theorists, a "system" was the combination of several intervals. The systems larger than the tetrachord are formed by the association of two or more tetrachords connected either by conjunction (*synemmenoi*), when the last note of a tetrachord coincides with the first note of the next, or by disjunction (*diezeugmenoi*), when the two tetrachords are separated by the interval of a tone. Thus, the association of two conjunct tetrachords constitutes a system of seven notes (*heptachordon*), and the association of two disjunct tetrachords a system of octave (*dia pason* or *harmonia*, according to the Pythagoreans: cf. Nicom. *Ench.* 9, p. 252, 11 Jan):

			Oktachordon System
Heptachordon System			**(Dia Pason, Harmonia)**
ti_1	*hypate*	mi	*hypate*
do_1	*parhypate*	fa	*parhypate*
re_1	*lichanos*	sol	*lichanos*
mi_1	*mese*	la	*mese*
fa_1	*trite*		
sol_1	*paranete*	ti	*paramese*
la_1	*nete*	do_1	*trite*
		re_1	*paranete*
		mi_1	*nete*

The names given the notes do not indicate acuteness of sound in the absolute, but relations between one note and another within the system: (1) *hypate* (scil. *chorde*) was "the highest, the extreme" chord because farthest from the player's body; (2) *parhypate* was the chord "next to the *hypate*"; (3) *lichanos*, the chord touched by the "index finger"; (4) *mese*, the "middle" chord; (5) *paramese*, the chord "next to the *mese*"; (6) *trite*, the "third" chord beginning from the highest; (7) *paranete*, the chord "next to the *nete*"; (8) *nete*, the "last," insofar as it was added later than the others; it was at the interval of an octave from the *hypate*. The note which in perfect systems is added below the lowest, before the *hypate*, is called *proslambanomenos*, the "added" sound (cf. Aristid. Quint. *De mus.* 1.6, p. 7, 15 ff. W.-I.).

The association of three conjunct tetrachords with a note added to before the lowest (*proslambanomenos*) constitutes the *systema teleion elatton*, the "lesser perfect system," while the association of two pairs of conjunct tetrachords separated by a tone of disjunction, with the addition of a note before the lowest (*proslambanomenos*), represents the *systema teleion meizon*, the "greater perfect system":

Lesser Perfect System		**Greater Perfect System**	
la	*proslambanomenos*	la	*proslambanomenos*
ti	*hypate hypaton*	ti	*hypate hypaton*
do_1	*parhypate hypaton*	do_1	*parhypate hypaton*
re_1	*lichanos hypaton*	re_1	*lichanos hypaton*
mi_1	*hypate meson*	mi_1	*hypate meson*
fa_1	*parhypate meson*	fa_1	*parhypate meson*
sol_1	*lichanos meson*	sol_1	*lichanos meson*
la_1	*mese*	la_1	*mese*
ti_{1b}	*trite synemmenon*	ti_1	*paramese*
do_2	*paranete synemmenon*	do_2	*trite diezeugmenon*
re_2	*nete synemmenon*	re_2	*paranete diezeugmenon*
		mi_2	*nete diezeugmenon*
		fa_2	*trite hyperbolaion*
		sol_2	*paranete hyperbolaion*
		la_2	*nete hyperbolaion*

The three tetrachords which compose the lesser perfect system are respectively specified (from the deeper to the more acute) by the genitives *hypaton, meson,* and *synemmenon* ("of the conjunct sounds"; cf. Cleon. *Isag.* 10, p. 200, 10 ff. Jan). The four tetrachords which compose the greater perfect system are designated, lowest to highest, by the following genitives: *hypaton, meson, diezeugmenon* ("of the sounds separated by the tone of disjunction"), *hyperbolaion* ("of the highest sounds").

The association of the two "perfect systems," the greater and the lesser, in a single succession of notes constitutes the *systema teleion ametabolon*, or "perfect immutable system":

Perfect Immutable System

la	*proslambanomenos*
ti	*hypate hypaton*
do_1	*parhypate hypaton*
re_1	*lichanos hypaton*

mi_1	*hypate meson*
fa_1	*parhypate meson*
sol_1	*lichanos meson*
la_1	*mese*
ti_{1b}	*trite synemmenon*
ti_1	*paramese*
do_2	*trite diezeugmenon* and *paranete synemmenon*
re_2	*paranete diezeugmenon* and *nete synemmenon*
mi_2	*nete diezeugmenon*
fa_2	*trite hyperbolaion*
sol_2	*paranete hyperbolaion*
la_2	*nete hyperbolaion*

The successions of sounds according to modern notation that I have given next to the ancient terms in the schemes of the different *systemata* should be regarded only as suggestions *exempli gratia*. We must remember that the ancient terms for the notes do not refer to sounds of set pitches, but rather indicate only the relative positions of the notes. It should also be recognized that the tetrachords constituting the systems are described in the diatonic genus only to facilitate the exposition. For example, the tetrachord of the *hypaton*, ti, do_1, re_1, mi_1 (diatonic), can also be read as ti, ti$\sharp$, do_1, mi_1 (enharmonic) or ti, do_1, $do_1\sharp$, mi_1 (chromatic). It is evident further from these considerations that no significance can be attributed to the Aristoxenian systems as regards actual musical practice. The absence of reference to concrete and real sounds suggests that these systems were conceived merely as abstract schemes of tetrachord successions, and as models—to be used only in theoretical research—of the disposition of the intervals within a space which extended to the double octave.

Within the greater perfect system, if we preserve the disposition of the intervals in the ascending succession of semitone, tone, tone (diatonic genus) in the constituent tetrachords, and if we consider only the four tetrachords conjunct two by two, without the *proslambanomenos* sound, we can identify seven *eide tou dia pason*, or "species of octave" (cf. Cleon. *Isag.* 9, pp. 197–98 Jan):

ti	$-$ ti$_1$	Mixolydian	intervals	St, T, T, St, T, T, T
do$_1$	$-$ do$_2$	Lydian		T, T, St, T, T, T, St
re$_1$	$-$ re$_2$	Phrygian		T, St, T, T, T, St, T
mi$_1$	$-$ mi$_2$	Dorian		St, T, T, T, St, T, T
fa$_1$	$-$ fa$_2$	Hypolydian		T, T, T, St, T, T, St
sol$_1$	$-$ sol$_2$	Hypophrygian		T, T, St, T, T, St, T
la$_1$	$-$ la$_2$	Hypodorian		T, St, T, T, St, T, T

In Cleonides' treatise, the description of the *eide tou dia pason* follows those of the *eide tou dia tessaron* and the *eide tou dia pente* — i.e., of the tetrachords and pentachords, which differ only in the position of the *pyknon* in the enharmonic and chromatic genera and of the semitone in the diatonic genus. In the case of the tetrachord, some modern scholars have chosen to distinguish a Dorian *eidos*, with initial semitone or *pyknon;* a Phrygian *eidos*, with semitone or *pyknon* in the middle; and a Lydian *eidos*, with semitone or *pyknon* at the end. Such a terminology is, however, entirely arbitrary and nowhere confirmed by ancient testimony. The names of the Dorian, Phrygian, and Lydian species of octave, which repeat at least partially those of the old harmoniae, have suggested that the two can be identified. A passage from Aristoxenus seems to corroborate this view (*Harm.* 2.36, p. 46, 10 Da Rios), but the evidence it provides is suspicious because the text has been corrected by R. Westphal through an intervention whose necessity is hard to justify. In the passage in question, Aristoxenus says that "our predecessors said nothing about what is in agreement and what is in contrast with the laws of music, and some of them did not even try to identify the differences among systems—they only examined the heptachords themselves (*peri auton monon ton heptachordon*), which they called *harmoniai;* others, on the other hand. . . ." Aristoxenus was certainly referring just to the different tunings (*harmoniai*) of seven-string instruments. This interpretation is confirmed by a passage of Aristotle (*Met.* 1093a14), which explicitly states *hepta de chordai he harmonia,* "seven strings constitute the *harmonia*," i.e., the "tuning." Westphal, on the other hand, has corrected Aristoxenus's phrase to *peri auton monon ton hepta oktachordon,* arbitrarily inserting the reference to the species of octave. Moreover, there is no analogy between the disposition of the intervals in the species of octave and in the schemes handed down by Aristides Quintilianus of the harmoniae with the same names. It is most probable that the names of the harmoniae were referred to the species of octave at a time when the first had already fallen into oblivion.

The same names were attributed to some of the *tonoi* or *tropoi*. These are scales of transposition obtained by Aristoxenus, who assigned the value of a musical note to the *chordai* of the perfect immutable system and transposed the resulting scale of two octaves by one semitone at a time for all the semitones included in an octave, for a total of thirteen scales (cf. Aristid. Quint. *De mus.* 10, p. 20, 10 W.-I.; Cleon. *Isag.* 12, p. 203, 6 Jan). The successors of Aristoxenus added another two tones to the acute so as to obtain fifteen tones. Of these, the five at the center had simple names (*dorios, iastios, phrygios, aiolios, lydios*); the five of lower pitch had names compounded with the prefix *hypo-* (*hypodorios*, etc.) and were placed at the interval of a fourth with respect to the corresponding *tonoi* with simple names; the five *tonoi* of higher pitch had names compounded with the prefix *hyper-* (*hyperdorios*, etc.) and also stood at the interval of a fourth in relation to the corresponding *tonoi* with simple names:

hypodorios	fa	$-$ fa_2
hypoiastios	fa♯	$-$ fa_2 ♯
hypophrygios	sol	$-$ sol_2
hypoaiolios	sol♯	$-$ sol_2 ♯
hypolydios	la	$-$ la_2
dorios	la♯	$-$ la_2 ♯
iastios	ti	$-$ ti_2
phrygios	do_1	$-$ do_3
aiolios	do_1 ♯	$-$ do_3 ♯
lydios	re_1	$-$ re_3
hyperdorios	re_1 ♯	$-$ re_3 ♯
hyperiastios	mi_1	$-$ mi_3
hyperphrygios	fa_1	$-$ fa_3
hyperaiolios	fa_1 ♯	$-$ fa_3 ♯
hyperlydios	sol_1	$-$ sol_3

The fifteen *tonoi* could have the constituent tetrachords in the forms corresponding to the three genera—diatonic, chromatic, or enharmonic. Alypius's models of notation are precisely organized in five triads of tonoi (*lydios, hypolydios, hyperlydios,* etc.) in the diatonic genus, and in five triads each also in the chromatic and enharmonic genera. Beside these very accurate names in the subdivision of the groups of *tonoi* (simple, with *hypo-, hyper-*), Aristides Quintilianus (*De mus.* 1.10, p. 20, 9 W.-I.) and Cleonides (*Isag.* 12, p. 203, 7 Jan) record others that are probably older and almost certainly Aristoxenian: *Hypophrygios barys* for the *Hypoiastios, Hypolydios barys* for the *Hypoaiolos, Phrygios barys* for the *Iastios, Lydios barys* for the *Aiolios, Mixolydios barys* for the *Hyperdorios, Mixolydios oxys* for the *Hyperiastios,* and finally *Hypermixolydios* for the *Hyperphrygios.* We notice that these terms, which we assume to be Aristoxenian, include only the names that recur in the list of the species of octave, and not any of the others.

We do not have a clear sense of the significance and value in musical theory and practice of the species of octave and of the thirteen—later fifteen—Aristoxenian and post-Aristoxenian *tonoi* in the order and with the names we know for them. If one considers that the difference among the various species of octave is determined merely by the disposition of the intervals of tone and semitone, they should be regarded as true modes, like our "major" and "minor," which differ from one another on account of the different position of the semitone intervals within the octave scale. But in order to be able to speak of modes in the modern sense with reference to ancient Greek music, one should identify in each species of octave a note with the characteristic of the tonic note in our tonal system—a note, that is, which represents the tonal basis of the entire octave.[6] Two pseudo-Aristotelian *Problems* (19.20; 36) and a passage of Claudius Ptolemy (*Harm.* 2.11, p. 65, 3 Düring) appear to suggest that the ancients may have attributed this role to the *mese.* However, in the *eidos Mixolydion* and in the *Hypolydion,* for example, the *mese* coincides with the first movable note of the enharmonic and chromatic *pyknon,* and given the variable character of its tonal position, we must rule out that it could represent the point of tonal attraction for all the other notes of the scale. The subdivision of the octaves into fourths and fifths has the purpose of identifying the tonic note at the meeting point between the one and the other, or of distinguishing authentic modes (Mixolydian, Phrygian, and Dorian) from imitative ones (Hypolydian, Hypophrygian, and Hypodorian), according to the positions occupied by the tetrachord and the pentachord; however, such subdivision is entirely arbitrary—there is no ancient evidence of this practice— and does not lead to probable results for a definition of modality and tonality. It represents nothing more than an attempt to inject the concepts of modality, typical of church music during the Late Middle Ages, into ancient musical doctrine. We should not forget in this respect that the basic system of Greek music was not the octave, but the tetrachord. A musical theory based on principles of tonality and modality, involving a particular hierarchy of notes and a certain disposition of the intervals within the octave, cannot therefore be easily assumed. In Greek musical practice, what especially counted was the genera—namely, how the intervals were arranged within the tetrachords and whether the latter were combined so as to be conjunct or disjunct.

Modal elements were certainly present in the old *harmoniae,* each of which conveyed a particular *ethos,* but their nature is hard to define because of the lack of ancient testimony on the subject. In the case of the octave species it is harder still: these are so mechanically determined and structured within the double octave of the greater perfect system as to suggest that for Aristoxenus and his followers they were abstract theoretical models of associations of intervals. We cannot even make them correspond to the successions of notes we find in the extant musical documents. The same observations are all the more valid when applied to the Aristoxenian *tonoi,* in which the disposition of the intervals remains always the same and the differentiating element consists only in the relative acuteness of the sounds, since each *tonos* proceeds from a semitone in the acute with respect to the preceding *tonos.* In the structure of the *tonoi* the genera of the tetrachords assume particular relevance: the scales of Alypius, which are modeled according to the scheme of the fifteen post-Aristoxenian *tonoi,* record for each tone the notes pertaining to the three genera—diatonic, chromatic, and enharmonic. Claudius Ptolemy, on the other hand, considers only seven *tonoi* (*Harm.* 2.9, pp. 60 ff. Düring), whose number and names correspond to those of the species of octave: Mixolydios, Lydios, Phrygios, Dorios, Hypolydios, Hypophrygios, and Hypodorios, from the highest to the lowest. (In the species of octave, however, the same names in the same order designate the *eide* from the lowest to the highest.) Ptolemy seems to attribute to each of these *tonoi* a modal value and to assign to their respective *mesai* a preeminent position among the notes of the *tonos,* since the melodic lines touch them with greater frequency than other notes (*Harm.* 2.11, p. 65, 3 Düring). It is evident that the seven Ptolemaic and the fifteen post-Aristoxenian *tonoi* have in common only the name and the extension (two octaves). We must not forget that Aristoxenus and Ptolemy lived five centuries apart.

The collocation of all the notes included within the range of two octaves plus a tone in a series of forty-five scales (fifteen per genus) modeled on the scheme of the immutable perfect system certainly derived from a theoretical requirement of classification as well as from the practical necessity of an orderly disposition of the two musical systems for the benefit of composers. One can therefore understand why the theorists of later times were not receptive to the Ptolemaic *tonoi,* which covered only a part of the tonal range, while Alypius, at the end of the Roman age (in the fourth to fifth century), was still basing his *Isagoge* on Aristoxenian schemes that went back seven centuries.

Ancient theoretical treatises reserve but little space to *melopoiia,* that is, the doctrine of musical composition. Cleonides (*Isag.* 13, p. 206, 3 ff. Jan) limits himself to distinguishing the *ethe,* the characteristics of melopoeia: the *diastaltikon,* magnificent and heroic, typical of tragedy; the *systaltikon,* subdued and unmanly, typical of erotic songs, *threnoi,* and lamentations; the *hesuchastikon,* serene and calm, of encomia and paeans. The four modes in which melody is realized, according to Cleonides, are the *agoge,* the *ploke,* the *petteia,* and the *tone.* The first of these is the development of melody by conjunct degrees; the second is "a parallel disposition of the intervals," probably a musical line consisting of sounds that are not contiguous but rather arranged according to regular intervals; the third is the repetition of a note; the fourth consists in lingering for a prolonged stretch of time on a position of the voice. A broader and more detailed treatment of melody is found in Aristides Quintilianus (*De mus.* 1.12, p. 28, 10 ff. W.-I.). He distinguishes, according to the pitches of the sounds employed, a *melopoiia hypatoeides*, a *mesoeides*, and a *netoeides*. The parts of melopoeia are the *lepsis*, the choice of the starting sound of the melody; the *mixis*, through which we combine the various tones of the voice, the systems, and the genera; and the *chresis*, which is the elaboration of the melody whose aspects are the *agoge*, the *petteia*, and the *ploke*, mentioned also by Cleonides. For each of these last three items, Aristides provides more complex and precise definitions than Cleonides. The *agoge* has three aspects: the *eutheia*, or "direct," which carries the voice by consecutive steps toward the high tones; the *anakamptousa*, "that which retraces its steps," which carries the voice in the same way toward the deeper tones; and the *peripheres*, "revolving," which progresses toward the acute by consecutive steps and toward the low by disjunct steps. The *petteia* is the most important aspect of the *chresis*. From it we know which sounds we must leave aside, which ones we should use and how many times, and from which ones we should begin and end. The *petteia* also defines the *ethos* of the melody.

There are three *tropoi*, or modes, of melopoeia according to genus: the nomic (of high pitch), the dithyrambic (of medium pitch), and the tragic (of low pitch). More numerous are the modes according to *eidos*, or form, such as erotic, epithalamian, comic, and encomiastic. Thus the melopoeiae differ according to their *genos* (enharmonic, chromatic, or diatonic), according to the system (acute, medium, or low pitch), according to the *tonos* (Dorian, Phrygian, etc.), according to *tropos* (nomic, dithyrambic, and tragic), and finally according to the *ethos*. With respect to the latter we distinguish a melopoeia *systaltike*, which arouses feelings of grief; a *diastaltike*, which shakes the soul; and a *mese*, which brings it back to serenity. We find a few references to melopoeia also in three anonymous treatises published by F. Bellermann (*De mus.* 3.83 ff., p. 28, 1 Najock), which merely list and define some technical terms: *prolepsis* (transition from a deep to an acute sound), *eklepsis* (the opposite transition, from an acute to a deep sound), *prokrousis* (two notes in a single beat, from the deep to the acute), *ekrousis* (two notes in a single beat from the acute to the deep), *ekrousmos* (transition from a deep to an acute sound and return to the deep), *kompismos* and *melismos* (repetition of a sound), *teretismos* (double repetition).

It is evident from what I have just said that with regard to melopoeia, all the elements which the sources provide are not sufficient to inform us about ancient techniques of composition. The data are very scanty and fragmentary, and it is impossible to determine to which period they refer. No musical examples are given.

The study of rhythm holds a position of great importance in ancient musical doctrines generally. That discipline considered the tempoes of the performance with regard not only to voice and sound but also to the movements of the body in dance. The earliest testimony concerning a theory of poetic and musical rhythm occurs in Plato's *Republic* (3.400a–c), and is ascribed to Damon. In the chapters which analyze the poetic and musical genres in order to establish which ones are suitable to the ideal state, Socrates begins the discussion of rhythms by premising that one should not seek *baseis* (i.e., dance "steps" or rhythms) that are varied and multiform but, rather, discover which rhythms pertain to an orderly and virtuous life. Once these have been identified, dance and song must be adapted to the words and not vice versa. Damon, in other words—or Plato, following Damon—did not accept that in musical compositions the rhythm or meter of the poetic text could be modified and deprived of its essential character by the rhythm of the melody and dance. He objected to the practice of violating the quantities of the syllables by lengthening them when they were short, or by protracting their length beyond the norm that one long equalled two shorts. In the dialogue with Socrates, Adimantus answers that he is unable to identify the rhythms to which his interlocutor is referring: he can only say, on the basis of his direct experience as spectator (*tetheamenos an eipoimi*), that there are three fundamental species (*eide*) of "steps" (*baseis*), just as in sounds there are four species on which all the *harmoniai* are based. Plato is here probably alluding to the four types of systems, with the intervals respectively arranged in the sequences St, T, T; T, St, T; T, T, St; T, T, T, which can be recognized in the first or in the last four notes of any octave (*harmonia*). We cannot think that he is referring either to the four notes of the tetrachord—he would not have used the term *eide*, "species"—or to the genera of the tetrachord—diatonic, enharmonic, and chromatic—which are three (if we do not count the *chroai*) rather than four. With regard to rhythm, the three species should be the iambic-trochaic (double genus), the dactylic-anapaestic (even genus), and the cretic-paeonian (hemiolion genus). This meaning of *eidos* in reference to the rhythmic pattern is confirmed by Aristides Quintilianus (*De mus.* 1.14, p. 34, 15 ff. W.-I.), who in connection with the *aloga* rhythmic patterns, maintains that they preserve "the analogies," the continuity in the general disposition of strong and weak beats on the basis of the numbers, that is, according to the duration of the syllables rather than according to the rhythmic species (*eide rhythmika*). The latter must therefore refer to the three genres of rhythm: even, double, and hemiolion.

In Plato's passage, Socrates postpones to a future discussion with Damon the task of establishing which rhythms express meanness and violence and which are suited to the opposite types of behavior. He believes that he has heard Damon speak of a compound enoplian, of a dactyl or heroon, with the thesis equal to the arsis and with the final syllable long or short, and finally of an iamb and a trochee, in which he associated short and long beats. For some of these rhythms, Damon criticized or praised the "tempos" of execution of the feet, as well as the rhythms themselves, or sometimes both together (for the value of *agoge* cf. Arist. Quint. *De mus.* 1.19, p. 79, 26 W.-I.).[7] From this particularly important passage for the history of the study of rhythm, we can derive precise data on Damon's doctrine. Damon already distinguished rhythms according to their genres (dactyl and heroon of the even genre, iamb and trochee of the double genre, the compound enoplian of the mixed genre, which includes feet of both the even and the

95

double genre). He took the tempos of performance (*agogai*) of the composition into account, and although this testimony is not directly referred to him, he evaluated rhythms—as well as harmoniae—on the basis of his experience as listener and spectator. What is surprising is that beside the mention of dactyls, iambs, and trochees, some reference should not be made also to feet of the hemiolion genre (with the ration 3 : 2 between strong and weak beats), such as cretics, paeons, and bacchii. We must consider, however, that Plato is dealing with the subject of rhythms within a broad context which does not allow him to go into too much detail. In this particular case, moreover, the author wants to give the impression that he remembers only the main points of Damon's speeches, and vaguely at that (*oimai . . . ou saphos . . .* , etc.). I do not believe, on the other hand, that we can advance the hypothesis that the rhythms of the hemiolion genre are not mentioned here because they were not suitable for being accepted into the Platonic state: they were, after all, the rhythms characteristic of Apollinean paeans.

Thus, by the middle of the fifth century B.C. the doctrine of rhythm had already assumed a distinct outline which will be preserved in its entirety by the scholar who gave this doctrine its definitive shape, Aristoxenus. In his *Rhythmic Elements,* Aristoxenus first of all made sure to define rhythm ("the arrangement of times," p. 15 Pighi = p. 3 Westphal), its mediums ("the poetic text, the melody, the movement of the body," p. 19 Pighi = 7, 15 W.), its unit of measure ("the primary time," simple and indivisible, p. 19 Pighi = 7, 21 W.). He then considers the elements of rhythm—the feet—and the ratios between strong and weak beats within them, and recovers the Damonic doctrine of the genres. Aristoxenus accepts as eurhythmic the feet of the equal, double, and hemiolion genres; he also, however, analyzes irrational feet (*alogoi*), namely those in which the ratio between the strong and the weak beat is halfway between two definite ratios—for example, between 2 : 1 and 2 : 2—such as the *choreios alogos,* which is halfway between the trochee and the spondee (p. 22 Pighi = 10, 19 W.). There are seven areas of possible difference between two feet: size, rhythmic genre (double, equal, hemiolion), irrationality (if one is *alogos* and the other is not), composition (if one is composed of two or more elements and the other is simple), subdivision (the possible ways in which strong and weak beats are subdivided within the feet, by number and measure), scheme (when the same parts of the same size are not arranged in the same order), and opposition (the position within the feet of the strong with respect to the weak beat, and vice versa).

After Aristoxenus, rhythmic doctrine did not change in its basic outline, but only became enriched with some details. In the first book of the *De musica* Aristides Quintilianus adds interesting observations to the Aristoxenian theory, which he organically expounds in the chapters devoted to the theories of the *symplekontes* (*De mus.* 1.13–17, pp. 31–38 W.-I.). The latter are those who had made no distinction between meters and rhythms, since in the musical practice down to the time of Timotheus the quantities of the metrical text had essentially provided the rhythmic basis for all vocal and instrumental performances (see above, p. 36). In addition to the three genres based on the even, double, and hemiolion ratios, Aristides considers the epitrite (3 : 4) as an eurhythmic ratio. He distinguishes between the rhythms composed *kata syzygian* (consisting of two simple and unequal rhythms) from those *kata periodon* (consisting of several rhythms). Besides simple and compound rhythms, he examines mixed rhythms, which can be subdivided by beats or rhythms: a rhythm of six beats can be divided in a strong beat of three and a weak beat of three (it will then belong to the equal genre, 3 : 3), or in two simple rhythms (2 : 1, 2 : 1; or 1 : 2, 1 : 2), in which case it will belong to the double genre. Among simple rhythms, Aristides lists the orthios and the trochee *semantos*—the first with four rising beats and eight falling ones, and the second with eight falling and four rising—and the paeon *epibatos* of ten beats—two falling, two rising, four falling, and two rising. These entries are an evident sign of a new evaluation, in musical performance, of the quantities of the syllables, which were no longer bound to traditional prosodic values of short and long, and whose duration could be lengthened to as many as eight primary times as a consequence of the variations of the *agoge*, or tempo of performance (cf. *Exc. Neap.* 15, p. 415, 3 Jan). In spite of

97

these additions and specifications, the fundamental lines of Aristo-xenus's doctrine remain unchanged and would do so until the end of the fifth century. Thus, the fact that Martianus Capella in the ninth book of his *De nuptiis Philologiae et Mercuri* faithfully trans-lated into Latin the most significant parts of the work of Aristides Quintilianus shows that he still believed in its essential value and importance.

Six

Texts with Musical Notation

The Notation

The theoretical treatises of Aristides Quintilianus (*De mus.* 1.11, pp. 24–27 W.-I.), Baccheius (*Isag.* 1.11, p. 293 Jan), Gaudentius (*Isag.* 22, p. 350 Jan), Alypius (*Isag.* 49, p. 368 Jan), and the Anon. Bellermann (3.66, p. 19 Najock) have preserved for us the signs of Greek notation, which are the same as those appearing in the few extant texts with musical notes. The most complete and organic collections are the tables of Alypius (p. 368 Jan), where the signs are arranged according to the double octaves of the fifteen *tonoi* in the diatonic, chromatic, and enharmonic genera. The notes appropriate to the Hyperphrygian (in part), Iastian, Hypoiastian, Hyperiastian, Dorian, Hypodorian, and Hyperdorian *tonoi* in the enharmonic genus have not been preserved, but the tables we possess and the testimony of other authors allow us to fill in the gaps. Greek notation included two different systems of signs, based on the letters of the alphabet, either in their normal form, or arranged horizontally, or upside-down, or with an added *apex*, or modified in their shapes. One system served to record the sounds of instrumental music, the other those of vocal music (cf. Arist.

Quint. *De mus.* 1.11, p. 23, 18 W.-I.; Gaud. *Isag.* 21, p. 350, 9 Jan; *Anon. Bell.* 3.68, p. 22, 1 Najock), but the texts that have been preserved do not reveal so precise a distinction. For example, of the two Delphic Hymns the first is accompanied by the signs of vocal notation and the second by those of instrumental notation, with no difference between the two in the use of the signs in relation to the literary text.

Modern scholars have expressed contrasting opinions on the origin and chronology of the two semiographic systems (see above, pp. 9–10). By the shape of the signs the instrumental system appears older than the vocal, whose notes consist in the letters of the Attic alphabet as it was reformed by the archon Euclid in 403 B.C. On the other hand, in the instrumental system the signs are arranged by triads, in which the straight sign (*orthon*) indicates the natural sound, the "distended" sign (*anestrammenon*) indicates the sound raised of one enharmonic or chromatic *diesis,* and the "inverted" sign (*apestrammenon*) indicates the sound raised of a second enharmonic or chromatic *diesis.* This arrangement suggests that a redefinition of the value of the signs occurred at the time when vocal notation was added to instrumental notation—i.e., certainly after 403 B.C. The vocal signs were arranged in triads in the simplest and more natural way, by assigning the three values of a note to three successive letters. For example, fa = Γ; fa♯ or ♯ (according to the genera) = B; and fa♯ or ♯♯ (according to the genera) = A, with a sequence of the signs from the acute to the deep. It is very probable that the signs of instrumental notation that were already in use for natural signs without accidentals were employed in a new triadic system which joined the already definitive system of vocal notation; this was done simply by modifying the position of the signs according to the altered value that had to be attributed to them.[1]

The following are the signs of the two systems, with the schema of the musical notes which are by convention taken as corresponding to each sign in the enharmonic genus (in the chromatic genus, the second note of the triad is raised by a semitone, the third by two):

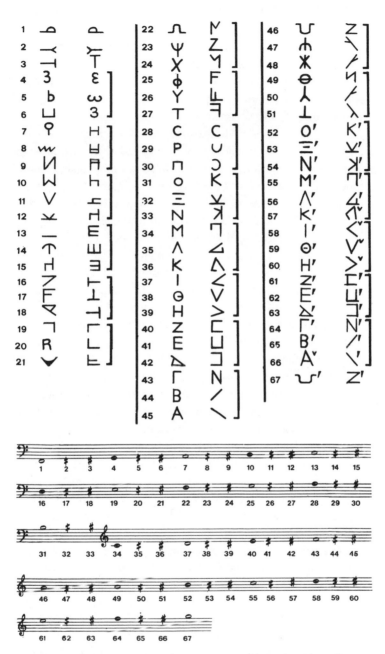

Figure 10. Vocal and instrumental notation systems, along with corresponding modern transcription.

We must allow that the double value of each of the two notes with accidentals (the second and third of each triad), according to the enharmonic and chromatic genus, can make the interpretation ambiguous. Fa♯, for example, is represented by the signs **B** (vocal) and ╱ (instrumental) in a chromatic tetrachord, and by the signs **Γ** (vocal) and **N** (instrumental) in an enharmonic tetrachord. Another fact should also be considered: the triadic arrangement does not take into account the difference between intervals of tone and intervals of semitone within the octave. Consequently, the sound corresponding to do_1 (or to ti♯) can be represented by the sound **M** (vocal) or **⅂** (instrumental), which represents do_1; by the sign **N** (vocal) or **Ӽ** (instrumental), which represents ti♯ in an enharmonic tetrachord; and by the sign **Ξ** (vocal) and **Ɯ** (instrumental), which represents ti♯ in a chromatic tetrachord. One can object that this observation is valid only in a tempered system, in which between ti♯ and do_1 there is no actual difference of pitch, while in a system of natural sounds the pitch of do_1 is higher than that of ti♯ by a minimal fraction of tone. In musical practice, however, infinitesimal intervals would certainly have been disregarded, as Aristoxenus's doctrine confirms, since it considers the interval of a semitone as equivalent to exactly half of the tone, and the enharmonic *diesis* as equivalent to the fourth part of the tone. This is not to say that Aristoxenus has anticipated by two millennia the theory of temperament of A. Werckmeister and J. S. Bach. The musical theory of Aristoxenus utterly ignores the concepts of tonality and harmony in the modern senses of the terms, concepts which gave rise at the end of the seventeenth century to the requirement of a subdivision of the octave into twelve identical semitones. Aristoxenus's motives for proposing the subdivision of the interval of a tone into two equal parts were very different— simpler, more elementary, and essentially practical.

In spite of the fact that the musical signs of the vocal and instrumental systems do not indicate duration, but only relative pitch, the inquiry as to the quantitative values to be assigned to each note could seem simple at first sight. In Greek vocal music, each syllable of the poetic text conveys, either by nature or by its position in the verbal chain, a temporal value of long or short, and this sequence of values constitutes the rhythmic basis of song. Any change of duration in a segment of such sequences of long and short syllables, and any peculiarity of performance is, or should be, marked in the texts by rhythmic signs. Most of these are illustrated and defined in the first and third anonymous treatises which Bellermann published in 1840 (1.1, p. 1; 3.102, p. 32 Najock). They are, as is well known, the *makra dichronos*, the long of two times (−); the *makra trichronos* (⌞), *tetrachronos* (⌣), and *pentachronos* (ɰ), longs of three, four, and five times, respectively; and the *chronos kenos brachys* (designated by the *leimma* in the two forms ∧ and ∩), the *chronos kenos makros* (⟑, ⋂̄), the *chronos kenos makros tris* (⟑̆, ⋂̆) and *tetrakis* (⟑̈, ⋂̈), i.e., the pauses of one, two, three, and four primary times, respectively. Finally, the *stigme* is a point placed above the musical note to mark, according to Anon. Bell. (1.3, p. 2 Najock), the beats in "arsis." Of course, as R. P. Winnington-Ingram has remarked, it is not clear whether we should understand "arsis" in the sense of "weak beat," according to the meaning given to the term until the late Roman period, or in the sense of "strong beat," such as we find in the treatises of Priscian (CGL 6, p. 521, 24 Keil) and Martianus Capella (p. 519, 17 Dick).[2] Other signs recurring in ancient texts are the *hyphen* and the *kolon*. The *hyphen*, an arc placed under two or three notes, is also cited but not clearly defined, in a passage of Anon. Bell. (3.86, p. 28 Najock): it should indicate a close link between two or three notes placed on the same syllable. The *kolon* is a double point whose function is not clear, but which probably was used alternatively to, or in conjunction with, the *hyphen* and also served to connect several notes placed on a single syllable able to define exactly the rhythmic schemes of the performances. However, when we go from the general statements to the analysis of individual texts, we perceive that the actual use of the signs is not always consistent, nor does it always agree with the definitions we derive from the treatises. Moreover, the texts often bear minute graphic symbols and reduplications of vowels which certainly affect the substance of rhythmic sequences, although they find no mention in the theoretical works.

The *leimma*, as I have said, is designated as a sign of pause (*chronos kenos*), but in Mesomedes (*Hymns* 4 and 5) in the edition by E. Pöhlmann, it cannot indicate a pause. The *leimma* always occurs on the penultimate long syllable of enoplians, ⌣–◡◡– ◡◡– –, which alternate with lines composed of three anapaests plus an iamb, ⌣–◡◡– ◡◡– ◡◡–. It is evident that in this case the sign is employed to increase the value of the syllable up to three times in order to equalize metrically unhomogeneous lines. An indirect proof of the validity of such interpretation is provided by lines 23 and 25 of *Hymn 4*: the penultimate syllable of these enoplians is tuned on three pitches (they represent the only cases in the *Hymns* in which we find three note signs on the same syllable). Also in these lines we remark an increase in the chronic value of the syllable. On the other hand, in the tragic text of *POslo* 1413 (first to second century) and in the Christian hymn of *POxy.* 1786 (third to fourth century), the *leimma* is always used to indicate the pause: the sign always occurs at the end of a sentence or syntactical period. In *POxy.* 2436 (first to second century), also a tragic text, the sign of *leimma* after a note indicates the lengthening of that note and of the corresponding syllable up to three time units, as in Mesomedes. In *PMich.* 2958 (second century), it denotes the lengthening of an already long syllable at line 1, of a lengthened short syllable at line 11, and of a short syllable at line 13; at lines 3, 4, 9, and 10, it marks a pause. In the paean *PBerlin* 6870 (second to third century), the sign is sometimes used at the end of a metrical period (lines 3, 5, 6, 9, 11, 12) to indicate a pause. Elsewhere (lines 4, 7, 8, 10, 17, 23), the *leimma* is found within a group of notes and is always connected to the note that follows by means of the *hyphen* (the only exception occurs at line 23). In these cases it certainly does not signify a pause. Similarly, at line 16, where the *leimma* is placed above the conjunction *kai*, it cannot be taken as a sign of pause. The *leimma* must therefore indicate a super-lengthening of the preceding syllable or of the syllable to which it is connected by the *hyphen*. In *POxy.* 3161, which has been recently published by M. W. Haslam in conjunction with 3162, the *leimma* is normally used to indicate a pause, but in two occurrences on syllables within a word (fr. 1, line 10; fr. 4, line 4) it can only signify the super-lengthening of the preceding syllable. I do not agree with Haslam, who also in these cases has interpreted the sign as pause.

In the case of the *leimma* we cannot, then, assume a homogeneous use of the sign in all the extant texts. We must, rather, attribute to it the value of pause or of lengthening of the note's duration on the basis of a careful study of each individual case even within the same document.

The lengthening of a syllable to three times—which in the *Hymns* of Mesomedes, as we have seen, is marked with the *leimma*—should be indicated by the *makra trichronos*. This is the sign ⌐, which occurs only in two ancient texts—*PWien* 29825c (third to second century B.C.), a fragment too small to reveal the rhythmic effects of such lengthening, and the Epitaph of Seikilos (Kopenhagen inv. 14897, first to second century). In the latter brief poetic text, the protraction of a few syllables causes the succession called a dochmius ($\smile - - - -$ = iamb + molossus) and of three lines consisting of choriamb plus bacchius ($\stackrel{\smile}{-}\smile\smile\stackrel{\smile}{-}\smile - -$), to become equivalent in measure to an iambic dimeter and three choriambic-iambic dimeters. But already in the Epitaph of Seikilos, beside the syllables marked with the *makra trichronos*, we find two other syllables—the penultimate of line 6, and the ultimate of line 11—of which the first is connoted by the presence of three notes, and the second by the presence of three notes connected by the *hyphen*, with a long sign (*makra dichronos*) on the second and third notes. These are certainly syllables that are brought to the measure of three times, as is required by the rhythmic correspondence among the values of the syllables in the four lines. Thus, the text shows three ways of indicating the same phenomenon—the protraction of a long syllable—a phenomenon which assumed considerable importance in Hellenistic and late Hellenistic music. The lengthening of short syllables is much less frequently attested in musical texts. Of the shortening of long syllables we find no trace, even though Dionysius of Halicarnassus (*De comp. verb.* 11, p. 64 Usener and Radermacher) attributes to music and rhythmics the possibility of both increasing and decreasing the quantity of the syllables.

The super-lengthening of a long syllable could also be indicated by the reduplication of the vowel, a phenomenon found especially in the most ancient texts, such as *PLeid.* inv. 510, *PWien* G 2315, *PWien* 29825a/b *verso*, and the two Delphic Hymns, one anonymous of 138 B.C. and the other by Limenius of 128 B.C. This practice could also be understood as a device for placing two note signs on the same syllable, with no significance with respect to rhythm. This is how E. Pöhlmann interprets it, so that in his transcription of the Delphic Hymns into modern notation, he attributes the value of a long—two time units—even to reduplicated vowels and diphthongs. In favor of the interpretation of the phenomenon as protraction of the duration of the syllables, we must certainly take into account the evidence provided by Aristophanes. In the *Frogs* (1314), as he criticizes the novelty of Euripidean songs, Aeschylus mentions the *eieieieieilissete* form, with a clear reference to the practice of modifying the duration of the initial syllable, in order that it might be sung with those melismas and flourishes of notes which appealed to contemporary audiences. At the rhythmic level, the chronic value of the syllable would thus be forced for the purpose of achieving special effects of expression. It is worth remarking in this connection that Schroeder, in his metrical analysis of Euripides' *Electra,* interprets the first syllable of *eilissomenos* at line 437 as five times long.

To return to the Delphic Hymns, the meter of both compositions is the cretic-paeonian, with the exception of the last part of the hymn of Limenius, which constitutes a prosodion in glyconics and free dimeters, separated from the preceding paean by the *paragraphos,* a horizontal bar in the margin. The reduplication of the vowel is found occasionally, but only in the cretic-paeonian parts. It is significant that in the two hymns there appear no rhythmic signs of any kind, which again suggests that the reduplication here replaces the rhythmic semiography. If the hypothesis that such reduplications indicate protraction is valid, the syllables are here protracted up to the measure of four times whenever the long vowel is repeated, and of three times when the short vowel is repeated. The hemiolion rhythm of the cretic, in which strong and weak beats alternate according to the ratio 3:2 or 2:3, would thus be protracted to the measure of the diiamb (3:3), or, more rarely, of the ditrochee or choriamb (*Anon.*, col. 1, line 12; *Limenius*, lines 13–14).

One naturally wonders why super-lengthenings do not occur in any regular manner and appear in the texts with a seemingly casual frequency. In all likelihood such rhythmic progression was determined mainly by the requirement of adapting the poetic text to a rather involved and complex melodic sequence, consistent with the habit prevalent in Hellenistic Greek music of adapting words to music rather than music to words.

We should remark, in connection with the lengthening of the cretic and paeon, that Heliodorus, a metricologist of the first century A.D. (*Sch.* Chaerob. ad Hephaest. 13, p. 247, 11 Consbr.), approved of the diaeresis at the end of each foot in cretic sequences because, with the empty time of the pause, it permitted a reading of the cretic (3:2) according to the six time scheme of the trochaic dipody (3:3). The anonymous author of the treatise on rhythmics of the *POxy.* 9 + 2687 (*POxy.* 34, p. 15 ff.), in the analysis of a lyric text, considers precisely the different issues of the cretic which result from the protraction of the first or second long syllable.

Yet another sign whose interpretation is controversial is the *makra dichronos*, placed on long syllables as in *PWien* G 2315—the papyrus of Euripides' *Orestes*—where it is found on the third from the last syllable of each dochmius. The sign also appears on long syllables in *PBerlin* 6870 (lines 9, 10, 11), in *POxy.* 1786 (lines 2, 3, 4, 5), and several times in *POslo* 1413, *POxy.* 2436, *PMich.* 2958, and *POxy.* 3161. In the case of the Berlin paean, Pöhlmann in his transcription interprets the sign as doubling the value of the long. In the case of *POxy.* 1786, on the other hand, Pöhlmann leaves the value of the long syllable unchanged, no doubt in order to preserve the anapaestic rhythm; he does the same in the case of *POxy.* 2436, of trochaic rhythm. The interpretation of the sign as indicating merely the presence of a long syllable is followed by R. P. Winnington-Ingram for the occurrences in *POslo* 1413. In the case of *PMich.* 2958, Winnington-Ingram does not in his commentary take a decisive position, but in his transcription he takes into account only the quantity of the syllables according to the poetic text and in practice does not assign the *makra dichronos* any particular value.[3] By contrast, Haslam, in his transcription of *POxy.* 3161 (pp. 65–67), attributes to the notes the beats which the rhythmic notation indicates, without taking the quantity of the syllables into account: he considers as long only those syllables marked with the *makra dichronos.* This subjective assessment does not appear plausible because it neglects the metrical element, which alone can provide an entirely reliable basis for identifying the musical rhythm.

The interpretation of the phenomenon is, as is apparent, far from univocal. To apply an identical parameter for the interpretation of the sign to all the texts is practically impossible. We must base ourselves on the very function which rhythmic signs were meant to fulfill: they served as warnings or reminders to the performer that he had to assign certain measures of duration to some syllables and not to others. Now, as we know from ancient and late antique sources (*Excerpta Neap.* 14–22, pp. 414–18 Jan; Dion. Hal. *De comp. verb.* 17.109, p. 71; 20.142, p. 92 Usener and Radermacher), in performance the duration of the syllables was not constant, but rather, varied according to the *agoge,* the tempo of diction, and in general according to the character and the requirements of the text. In any given word, a long syllable could also be rendered with a longer or shorter duration than a normal long. Thus, a plausible interpretation of apparently useless signs, such as the *makra dichronos,* is that it warned the performer not to decrease the quantity of the syllable below two beats, but to emphasize its length in diction or song.

The groupings of several notes on a single syllable and the rhythmic signs such as the *makra dichronos,* the *leimma,* the *hyphen,* and the *kolon* would require a more lengthy discussion. Their significance must necessarily be researched by induction, since there is no reference to the subject in the ancient music treatises. Only from a comparison of different groups of signs can we derive indications as to the chronic value of the syllables on which they are placed. Here an analysis of such groupings would take too much time. I only wish to remark that the pattern of interpretation proposed by E. Pöhlmann for *PBerlin* 6870—the paean whose text consists exclusively of long syllables—cannot be valid for other documents.[4] The application of Pöhlmann's pattern would, in fact, involve the subdivision of the *chronos protos,* which Aristoxenus and all the later scholars of rhythm regard as the smallest and indivisible temporal unit. This is the case with *POxy.* 1786 (lines 3, 4, 5), *POslo* 1413 (lines 2a, 16, 18), *POxy.* 2436 (col. 2, lines 3, 4, 5, 8) and *PMich.* 2958 (lines 7, 9). On the other hand, I do not believe that we can assume for ancient music the same isomensural rigor and the same respect for regularity in the succession of beats which characterize modern Western music. I do not think, for example, that for ancient compositions we can hypothesize the use of the triplet, which is never attested in the ancient sources.

We must recognize that it is not possible to base our evaluation of rhythmic signs on preconceived patterns valid for all the documents, even if such patterns are founded on ancient definitions of the value of the signs. We must always remember that between the earliest and the latest ancient musical texts there intervenes a period of about seven hundred years. Over such a long span of time, the writing of music, especially with respect to rhythm, underwent considerable evolution. For example, the reduplication of a long vowel or a diphthong is a recurrent phenomenon in the earliest texts, but becomes much rarer, or even disappears altogether, in the most recent ones. On the other hand, the rhythmic semiography became ever more complex and detailed as time passed. This was due to the need of a later age to annotate subdivisions of times, links, pauses, and the like, which characterized a musical discourse more varied and richer in melismas. What is certain is that in antiquity musical writing did not represent a means for promulgating musical compositions, such as the printing and selling of musical scores in our time. It forever remained confined to a narrow milieu of professionals who employed it mostly for marking the elements that could be useful to them for a correct execution.

The comparison between an ancient musical text and a modern score suggests yet another thought. Because of the demands of harmony and polyphony, the musicians of our recent past—until the beginning of this century—have been careful to seek homogeneity of rhythm and regularity of beats in compositions which have been rigorously mensural. In ancient Greek music, which was based only on melody, just as the pitch of certain notes (the inner notes in the tetrachord) could be varied at will by the composer-performer, so also the tempo and the duration of the syllables within the foot must have been subject to unlimited increases and reductions. Starting from the second half of the fifth century, Greek music typically sought *metabolai*—rhythmic variations—which manifested themselves especially through pauses and protractions. Yet the meters of the poetic texts still guaranteed a certain rhythmic order. We cannot doubt the importance of the metrical chain for our rhythmic understanding of a musical passage. Surprising from this point of view therefore is the position taken by Haslam, who at the end of his commentary to *POxy*. 3162 (pp. 71–72) comes to admit only as *extrema ratio* that a short syllable with no rhythmic signs has a shorter duration than a long with no rhythmic signs; he then disregards this fact in his transcriptions into modern notation.

Texts with Musical Notes

The extant Greek texts with musical notation number twenty-three in all. With the exception of five, which were discovered later (*PLeid.* inv. 510 and *POxy*. 3161, 3162, 3704, and 3705), they are collected in the edition of E. Pöhlmann, which also contains Renaissance and modern falsifications on texts of ancient authors.[5] What follows is a list in chronological order.

1. *PLeid.* inv. 510.[6] Middle of the third century B.C. The lines of the text are intercalated with those of the notation. The first four include lines 1500–1509 of Euripides' *Iphigenia in Aulis;* the last four (the only ones readable), lines 784–92. The juxtaposition of the two passages in that order suggests that this was an anthological promptbook.[7] Oddly, vocal and instrumental notes occur on the same line and with the same function. There are also rhythmic signs, such as the *disema* (line 14.2) and the *stigme* (lines 10.1, 12.4, 12.5). The notes employed, if the interpretation of the signs is correct, are sol_2, $\#sol_2$, $\#la_2$, do_3, $\ddagger do_3$, $\#do_3$, re_3, $\ddagger re_3$, mi_3, fa_3, sol_3, $\#la_3$, almost all belonging to the Phrygian *tonos.*

[? ? I O Ж ⊥ Ʊ

[μή] τε ἐμοὶ μήτε ἐμοῖσ[ι τέκνων τέκνοις ἐλπὶς ἅδε ποτ' ἔλθοι

[. Τ [Τ _ Ш ?

[οἵαν] αἱ πολύχρυσοι Λυδαὶ[καὶ Φρυγῶν ἄλοχοι στήσουσι παρ' ἱστοῖς
μυθεύ<ου>σαι

? ? Λ _Ι. ? ⊥

τάδε ἐς ἀλλήλας· τίς ἄ[ρα μ' εὐπλοκάμου κόμας ἔρυμα δακρυόεν

Γ ⁻[? ⊥ ? ? [Τ Γ Τ

τ[αα]ς γᾶς πατ·ρίας ὀλο[μένας ἀπολωτιεῖ;

Figure 11. Euripides, *Iph. Aul.* 783–792: text and musical notation.

μήτε ἐμοὶ μήτε ἐμοῖσι

οἵαν αἱ πολύχρυσοι Λυδαὶ

τάδε ἐς ἀλλήλας · τίς α

ταας γᾶς πατ·ρίας ὀλομένας

Figure 12. Euripides, *Iph. Aul.* 783–792: text and modern musical transcription.

111

2. *PZenon* 59533 (n. 35, pp. 110 ff. P.). Third century B.C. A fragment of six lines, three of text and three of notation, perhaps belonging to a tragedy. The Ptolemaic sign of *sampi* (= 900) at the bottom of the fragment suggests the indication of the number of lines in the roll. The notes (do, $\flat$la, la, ti, do$_1$, $\flat$re$_1$, re$_1$, $\flat$mi$_1$) belong to the diatonic and chromatic Phrygian *tonoi,* but the signs Y and N, cut by the *makra dichronos,* cause problems of interpretation.

3. *PWien* G 2315 (n. 21, pp. 78 ff. P.). Third to second century B.C. Contains fourteen lines, seven of text, which reproduce lines 338–44 of Euripides' *Orestes,* as well as seven lines of notes intercalated in the text. Lines 338 and 339 are reversed with respect to the text of the manuscripts. The first line of the text contains the second *dochmius* of line 339 and the first of line 338, separated by the sign Ż which seems to indicate sol$_1$ in the instrumental notation. The second line contains the second *dochmius* of line 338 and the first of line 340, separated by the same sign Ż. The latter recurs in the fourth line of the notation, to separate the notes pertaining to the two *dochmii* of line 342 (line 4), and in the seventh line of the text between the two *dochmii* of line 344. Lines 5–6 of the text contain the two *dochmii* of line 343, each internally subdivided by the group of signs ‎ךٳ‎ . The first of these is a *diastole,* a sign of separation, and the other two are instrumental notes (fa and ti$_b$). Two signs of the rhythmic notation also appear— the *stigme* and the *makra dichronos.* In two cases (lines 6 and 7) we notice the reduplication of the vowel. The vocal notes (sol, la, la $\sharp$ or $\sharp$, ti$_b$ or ti, re$_1$, mi$_1$, mi$_1$ $\sharp$ or fa) belong to the enharmonic (or chromatic) and diatonic Lydian *tonoi.* They also recur, however, in the two Dorian and Phrygian scales (Platonic *harmoniai*) of Aristides Quintilianus (*De mus.* 1.9, p. 19 W.-I.). The interpretation of the notes and of the different signs is controversial.[8]

4–8. *PWien* 29825 a/b recto; a/b verso; c, d, f, 13763/1494 (pp. 22–29, pp. 84 ff. P.). Third to second century B.C. This is a series of papyrus fragments which were found with the *Orestes* papyrus. The first, in lyric anapaests, may belong to a tragedy. The others are too small to allow any hypothesis on their contents. Remarkable in *PWien* 29825 a/b *recto* is a direction of modulation (*Phrygisti*) on line 6 of the notes, as well as the sign 𝄪 in correspondence with line 6 of the text, indicating perhaps the attack of the chorus (*chorou*). In *PWien* 29825 a/b *verso* we find the *diastole* ⟩ (lines 3, 7), the direction *Lydisti* (line 11), and the reduplication of the diphthong (line 12); in *PWien* 29825c, the sign of *makra trichronos;* in *PWien* 29825f the *diastole* ⟩ followed by the instrumental note Γ (line 4 of the text); and finally, in *PWien* 13763/1494, the simultaneous presence of vocal and instrumental notes, the latter arranged on two lines independent of the poetic text (lines 2–3; p. 29, lines 3–4), and two rhythmic signs (*stigme* and *makra dichronos*).

9. Delphi inv. nr. 517, 526, 494, 499 (n. 19, pp. 58 ff. P.). 138 B.C. A paean in honor of Apollo by an anonymous Athenian author, preserved in an inscription that was placed on the southern wall of the Treasury of the Athenians at Delphi and was found in a fragmentary state. The inscription develops for 34 lines on two columns. There have been several proposals for its reconstruction, differing only with regard to the arrangement of the marginal fragments. The text is entirely in cretics, with frequent reduplications of vowels and diphthongs, which modify the normal rhythm through the insertion of iambic, trochaic, and choriambic rhythms. The use of the vocal notes bmi, sol, bla, bti, do_1, bre_1, re_1, bmi_1, fa_1, $bsol_1$, sol_1, bla_1, la_1, suggests the hypothesis of an introduction (lines 1–8) in the Phrygian *tonos*, perhaps according to the archaic model of the *spondeion*, with subsequent modulation to the Hyperphrygian (lines 8–16), and return to the Phrygian.[9] The tetrachords are of the diatonic and chromatic genera.

10. Delphi inv. 489, 1461, 1581, 209, 212, 226, 225, 224, 215, 214 (n. 20, pp. 68 ff. P.). 128 B.C. As the heading (cols. 1–2) indicates, this text includes a paean and a prosodion in honor of the god Apollo, composed and accompanied with the cithara by Limenius, the son of the Athenian Thoinos. This text is also preserved in an inscription of the Treasury of the Athenians at Delphi. It consists of 40 lines of text with instrumental notes. The first 33 lines, concluded by a *paragraphos*, contain the paean in cretics: the last seven constitute the prosodion in glyconics and choriambic dimeters. Reduplications of vowels and diphthongs are

Figure 13. Epitaph of Seikilos: ancient notation and modern transcription.

114

as frequent in the paean as in the anonymous Hymn, while they are completely lacking in the prosodion. The notes (mi, fa, sol, la, $\flat$ti, ti, do_1, re_1, $\flat mi_1$, mi_1, fa_1, sol_1, la_1, ti_1) belong to the Hypolydian and Lydian *tonoi,* with modulation to the Hyperlydian. The tetrachords are of the diatonic genus. Only the sequence la, $\flat$ti, ti, re is chromatic (Lydian *tonos*).

11. Kopenhagen inv. no. 14897 (n. 18, pp. 54 ff. P.). First century A.D. The Epitaph of Seikilos, inscribed on a funerary stele found in 1883 at Aidin near Tralles in Asia Minor and destroyed in 1922. It is composed of an elegiac distich without notes, a poem of four verses arranged on six lines with vocal notes and rhythmic signs *(makra dichronos, makra trichronos, stigme, hyphen),* and the final dedication "Seikilos, the son of Euterpos, lives." The *makrai dichronoi* and the groupings of three notes on one syllable protract to three beats some of the long syllables, thereby changing the rhythm of bacchius and spondee of the first line into that of the iambic dimeter, and the rhythms of the final bacchii of the remaining three lines into iambic rhythms. The vocal notes mi, $\sharp$fa, sol, la, ti, $\sharp do_1$, re_1, mi_1, belong to the diatonic Iastian *tonos.* The "species of octave" is Phrygian.

12. *POslo* 1413 (nn. 36–37, pp. 114 ff. P.). First to second century A.D. This papyrus consists of nineteen lines of text with musical notes of anapaestic rhythm (lines 1–15) and iambic rhythm (lines 15–19), and twelve small fragments. Text and notation seem to belong to the same hand. There are erasures and corrections, and a second line of musical notes has been added above the first (lines 2b, 3b; fr. c, line 3; fr. d, lines 1–2)—no doubt a new melody to replace the previous one. All these elements suggest that this is a composer's autograph text. The papyrus has also the surprising feature that musical notes are supplied for portions of the text that were normally just recited and not sung, such as the iambic trimeters of lines 15–19. The subject matter of lines 1–15 is the apparition of Achilles' ghost narrated to Deidameia by a witness. Lines 15–19 contain references to Lemnos, Hephaestus, and perhaps to the son of Achilles, Neoptolemus. In all likelihood this is an anthology of Hellenistic tragic texts.[10] Rhyth-

mic signs are frequent (*makra dichronos, stigme, hyphen, leimma,* and *kolon*). There are a few cases of reduplication of vowel or diphthongs (first syllable of proper names), and of *scriptio plena.* The vocal notes used at lines 1–15 (mi, ♯fa, sol, ♯sol, la, ti, do_1, ‡do_1, ♯do_1, re_1, fa_1) recur in the diatonic Iastian *tonos,* with the exception of ♯sol and ‡do, which belong to the diatonic Hypoiastian *tonos* and to the enharmonic Hyperiastian *tonos,* respectively. The vocal notes of lines 15–19 (mi, fa, sol, la, ♭ti, ti, do_1, re_1, mi_1) are found in the Lydian *tonos,* with the exception of ti, which occurs in the scheme of the Hypolydian *tonos.*

13. *POxy.* 2436 (n. 38, pp. 126 ff. P.). First to second century A.D. The fragment contains the end of a column (six extremely short lines), and the beginning of another (eight lines), consisting of verses where one recognizes iambic and cretic sequences. It is not possible to determine exactly to which poetic genre the fragment belongs. The hypothesis has been advanced that it may represent a monody from Euripides' *Meleager.*[11] It bears the sign of rhythmic notation (*makra dichronos, hyphen, stigme, kolon,* and *leimma*). The vocal notes (fa, sol, la, ♭ti, ti, do_1, re_1, mi_1, fa_1, sol_1) all occur in the diagram of the diatonic Hypolydian *tonos.*

14. *POxy.* 3704.[12] Second century A.D. Consists of three fragments written on the recto and on the verso, too small to reveal the poetic genre of the composition, probably of mythological subject (in fr. 1 verso, Typhos is quoted). The meter appears to be mostly dactylic (or anapaestic). The signs above the text belong to vocal notation and to rhythmic semiology. The vocal notes (sol, la, ti, do_1, re_1, mi_1) occur in Alypius's table of the diatonic Hyperionian. The sign ∩ is almost certainly to be interpreted as an upside-down Ω, which appears in the same table (sol_1). Because of the exiguity of the text, it is hard to determine how the rhythmic signs are used. The *disema* is placed over long syllables, with the only probable exception of fr. 1 recto, line 3, *ánomo.* The *leimma* ∩ is always accompanied by the *disema* and is always placed at word end. It can therefore signify either protraction of the value of the final syllable or a pause of two times. The text also bears signs of *stigme,* double point, and slanted bar, but their significance is uncertain.

15. *PMich.* 2958 (nn. 39–40, pp. 126 ff. P.). Second century
A.D. The fragment includes 26 lines of text with notation. Only line
5 consists exclusively of musical notes. A space between lines 18
and 19 separates a first part with notes of the Hyperiastian *tonos*
(sol, do_1, re_1, mi_1, ♯fa_1, sol_1) from a second part with notes of the
Hypolydian *tonos* (fa, sol, la, ti, do_1, re_1, mi_1). The state of the
fragment—only the right-hand side of the column is preserved—
does not allow us to determine with any accuracy the metrical
structure of the text, where iambs or trochees, and perhaps dochmii and cretics, seem to prevail. Rhythmic signs are present (*makra
dichronos, hyphen, stigme,* and *leimma*). Remarkable is the use (also
found in *POxy.* 3161, on the line of the musical notation only) of a
transverse bar (lines 14, 18), which cuts the lines of the text and
notation and which at line 14 coincides with the iatus. It is certainly a dramatic text (Aegisthus is named at line 17).

16. Mesomedes (nn. 1–5, pp. 13 ff. P.). Second century A.D.
Four of the hymns which tradition assigns to Mesomedes, a musician active at the court of Hadrian, have been handed down in
manuscripts with musical notation. The first is a proem to the
Muse in four verses, iambic dimeters alternated with iambic dimeters catalectic (enoplians). The second, a proem to Calliope and
Apollo, consists of two distichs (masc. *hemiepes* + enoplian) and
one lecythion. The third, a hymn to the sun, and the fourth, a
hymn to Nemesis, are in paroemiacs and anapaestic dimeters with
an iamb in place of the anapaest in last position. Signs of rhythmic
notation are used (*makra dichronos* and *leimma*). We notice the
presence of three notes over a single syllable, with consequent
lengthening of that syllable to three beats. The musical notes
belong to the Lydian *tonos* (mi, fa, sol, la, ♭ti, do_1, re_1, mi_1, fa_1,
sol_1).

17. *PBerlin* 6870 (nn. 30–33, pp. 94 ff. P.). Second to third
century A.D. Includes the following: a paean (lines 1–12), an instrumental fragment (lines 13–15), a passage from a tragedy (lines 16–
19), a second instrumental fragment (lines 20–22), and an isolated
verse (line 23), perhaps to be added to the tragic verses of lines 16–
19. The paean has long syllables exclusively. Its rhythm is certainly
modified by the presence of the *makra dichronos, leimma, hyphen,*

stigme, and *kolon,* and by the combination of several musical notes over a single syllable, but to attribute a protracted chronic value to the various syllables with rhythmic signs is extremely problematic. The musical notes (sol, la, ti, do_1, re_1, mi_1, $\sharp fa_1$, sol_1, la_1) belong to the Hyperiastian *tonos,* just like those of the instrumental fragments, whose melodies develop in the same tonal range. Here the rhythm, in the absence of the text, is determined by the presence of the same rhythmic signs as those appearing in the paean. In the tragic passage, the first verse (line 16) is introduced by a direction in the margin which probably marks the attack of the chorus (*all[o] ch[orou]*). Line 23 is also introduced by *al[lo].* It contains a reference to the death of Ajax, perhaps in connection with the judgment about Achilles' arms, since Odysseus is mentioned as well. The rhythm is prevalently dactylic or anapaestic, and rhythmic signs abound also here. The interpretation of the musical notes presents a few problems because some signs, such as the *apex,* should indicate sounds raised by an octave with respect to others. The notes employed seem to be $\sharp fa$, $\sharp sol$, ti, $\sharp do_1$, re_1, fa_1, $\sharp fa_1$, of the Hyperaeolian *tonos,* with the exception of fa_1, which appears in the Hyperiastian, Hypolydian, and Lydian *tonoi.*

18. *POxy.* 3136.[13] Third century A.D. Four fragments, not very significant because of the exiguity of the texts, which does not permit a certain definition of their genre. The latter, however, is probably dramatic, since the mentions of Paris (fr. 3, line 2), Scyros (fr. 2, line 13), and Achilles (fr. 2, line 16) bespeak an epic subject. Metrical analysis does not lead to certain results because the sequences are very brief. Rhythmic signs are frequent (*makra dichronos, stigme, hyphen, kolon,* and *leimma*). At any rate the interpretation of the editor is improbable because in his modern transcription he assigns chronic values to the syllables simply on the basis of the rhythmic signs pertaining to each, without taking quantity into account. The musical notes (re, mi, $\sharp fa$, sol, la, ti, do_1, $\sharp do_1$, re_1, mi_1, sol_1) belong to the Hypolydian *tonos* with the exception of $\sharp fa$ and $\sharp do_1$, which seem to indicate a modulation to the Iastian *tonos.* In fragments 1 and 4 we notice the presence of a transverse bar on the line of notation, a phenomenon of uncertain significance.

19. *POxy.* 3162.[14] Third century A.D. This fragment includes seven lines of text with musical and rhythmic signs (*stigme, makra dichronos*, and *kolon*). Its brevity prevents us from formulating any hypothesis with respect to genre. The rhythm appears to be iambic or trochaic. The musical notes are la, ti, do_1, re_1, mi_1, fa_1, of the Hypolydian *tonos*. Again in the case of this fragment we cannot accept the transcription into modern notation the editor proposes, since he fails to take the quantity of the syllables into account and considers as long only those syllables marked with the *makra dichronos*. Equally improbable is the hypothesis that triplets were used to reduce the duration of two notes on a single syllable (one of them with the *makra dichronos*) from three to two beats.

20. *POxy.* 3705.[15] Third century A.D. A brief phrase (*tou de topou mne-*) is written three times in three superimposed lines, over each of which we find musical signs of the vocal notation belonging to the diatonic Hypolydian *tonos* (la, ti♭, ti, do_1, re_1, mi_1, sol_1, la_1). What follows is a seventh line of musical signs only, which belong to the same group as the preceding ones. The sign V, for all that it occurs in Alypius's table of the diatonic Hypolydian, causes problems of interpretation. If we attribute to it the value of do in the lower octave with respect to $\overset{\cdot\cdot}{\Xi}$, M (do in the central octave), as Alypius's table prescribes, the fragment would then come to include intervals larger than an octave between consecutive notes—which is contrary to the practice of composition in all the other extant fragments. To identify other possible values for the V sign is on the other hand very problematic. The rhythmic notation is scanty. The *disema* occurs only once, over a long syllable (line 1, 1). The *hyphen* is used desultorily for connecting two notes over the same syllable. If two notes connected over the same syllable represent the chronic value of a long, the syllable *to-* of *topou* (line 2) is lengthened. The rhythm is iambic. We cannot determine to what type of composition the fragment belongs.

21. *POxy.* 1786 (n. 34, pp. 106 ff. P.). Third to fourth century A.D. A Christian hymn to the Trinity in five lines: the first three are mutilated in the first half, the fourth is almost whole, and of the fifth only the musical notation in the first half is extant. The rhythm is prevalently anapaestic. Rhythmic signs are present over

almost all the syllables (*machra dichronos, stigme, hyphen, kolon, leimma* of two beats). The musical notes (fa, sol, la, ti, do_1, re_1, mi_1, fa_1) belong to the Hypolydian *tonos*.

22. *Hormasia* (n. 6, pp. 32 ff. P.). Some manuscripts, where theoretical musical treatises are collected, include this text, which contains musical notes of uncertain date and of doubtful interpretation. It consists of a sequence of 32 pairs of vocal and instrumental signs. Sixteen pairs represent notes "of the left hand" (*aristeras cheiros*), sixteen "of the right hand" (*dexias cheiros*). In each pair the vocal sign is preceded by the letter O or A, the instrumental sign by the letter K (in correspondence to O) or M (in correspondence to A). The value of such symbols has not been so far interpreted with any certainty. Each pair of signs is also preceded by the indication of the position which the note occupies in the scale (*proslambanomenos, mese, nete,* etc.). The title (*He koine hormasia he apo tes mousikes metabletheisa Lydiou kata ton diatonon*) is difficult to interpret because the meaning of *hormasia* is uncertain. The term occurs only here, and is perhaps connected to *harmozo* through the attested form *hormazo* (*Et. M.* p. 631, 49 Gaisford). Clear, on the other hand, is the reference to the diatonic Lydian *tonos*, to which almost all the vocal and instrumental signs occurring in the text belong. The signs of lines 26–32 repeat those of lines 19–25 at the higher octave (with the addition of an *apex*). The two pairs which do not appear in the diatonic Lydian *tonos*, and which refer to the notes ti and do, belong to the diatonic Hypolydian *tonos*, as a marginal gloss at lines 17–26 indicates. None of the hypotheses that have been advanced concerning the interpretation of this document seem convincing.

23. *Anonymi Bellermann* par. 97–104 (nn. 7–12, pp. 36 ff. P.). Six pieces of instrumental music whose rhythm is indicated each time in the heading (*kolon hexasemon, allos hexasemos, tetrasemos, dodekasemos, allos dodekasemos, okto[kaideka]semos*), as well as by the presence of rhythmic signs (*makra dichronos* and *trichronos, stigme,* and *leimma* of one or two beats). All the notes belong to the diatonic Lydian *tonos*. There are no clues for dating the pieces.

Sources

The Hymn to Hermes

n the *Homeric Hymn to Hermes* music appears twice in the
foreground: at the beginning of the poem, when newborn
Hermes creates the lyre (lines 20–64), and at the end, when
Hermes, in order to placate Apollo, who is angered by the sly
theft of his fifty cows, offers Apollo the lyre as a gift (lines 416–
507). In the course of the narrative, Hermes twice intones his song,
accompanying himself with the new instrument. First he sings the
praises of his birth and house in an improvised poem "as young
men do at the time of feasts when they taunt and mock each other"
(lines 55–56). Later, he draws a broader picture, recounting the
origin of the cosmos and of the gods, among whom he attributes to
Mnemosyne (memory), the mother of the Muses, the highest
honor (lines 423–33). The two episodes respectively allude to two
very common musical genres of archaic Greece: the sympotic
song, composed on the occasion of feasts, and the hymn in honor
of the gods, based on a mythological repertoire committed to
memory and handed down by oral tradition. The dialogue between Hermes and Apollo, who is happy to accept the gift of the
lyre, contains meaningful references to the occasions of music and

song (the banquet, the dance, the feast), to the effects of music on
the listeners (in music are combined "three things to take all at
once—good cheer, love, and sweet sleep"), and, finally, to the didactic function of song and to the professional status of the singer:
the lyre "will teach . . . all manner of things joyful to the mind,"
when it is played "with a gentle touch" by "whoever with skill and
wisdom expertly asks."

TO HERMES

1 Of Hermes sing, O Muse, the son of Zeus and Maia,
    lord of Kyllene and Arcadia abounding with sheep,
    helpful messenger of the immortals, whom Maia bore,
    the fair-tressed and revered nymph, when she mingled in
      love
5 with Zeus; she shunned the company of the blessed gods
    and dwelt inside a thick-shaded cave, where Kronion,
    escaping the eyes of immortal gods and mortal men,
    mingled with the fair-tressed nymph in the darkness of
      night,
    while sweet sleep overcame white-armed Hera.
10 But when the mind of great Zeus accomplished its goal,
    and the tenth moon was set fast in the sky,
    a new-born saw the light, and uncanny deeds came to pass.
    Then she bore a child who was a shrewd and coaxing
      schemer,
    a cattle-rustling robber, and a bringer of dreams,
15 a watcher by night and a gate-keeper, soon destined
    to show forth glorious deeds among the immortal gods.
    Born at dawn, by midday he played his lyre,
    and at evening he stole the cattle of far-shooting Apollon,
    on the fourth of the month, the very day mighty Maia bore
      him.
20 After he sprang forth from his mother's immortal limbs,
    he did not remain for long lying in his holy cradle,
    but he leaped up and searched for the cattle of Apollon,

stepping over the threshold of the high-roofed cave.
There he found a tortoise and won boundless bliss,
25 for Hermes was the first to make a singer of a tortoise,
which met him at the gates of the courtyard,
grazing on the lush grass near the dwelling
and dragging its straddling feet; and the helpful son of
    Zeus
laughed when he saw it and straightway he said:
30 "Already an omen of great luck! I don't despise you.
Hail, O shapely hoofer and companion of the feast!
Your sight is welcome! Whence this lovely toy,
the gleaming shell that clothes you, a tortoise living on the
    mountains?
But I shall take you and bring you inside; you'll profit me.
35 And I shall not dishonor you for you will serve me first.
Better to be inside; being at the gates is harmful for you.
Indeed alive you shall be a charm against baneful
witchcraft; and if you die, your singing could be beautiful."
Thus he spoke and with both hands he raised it up
40 and ran back into his abode, carrying the lovely toy.
There he tossed it upside down and with a chisel of gray
    iron
he scooped out the life of the mountain-turtle.
As when swift thought pierces the breast
of a man in whom thick-coming cares churn,
45 or as when flashing glances dart from quick-rolling eyes,
so glorious Hermes pondered word and deed at once.
He cut measured stalks of reed and fastened them on
by piercing through the back the shell of the tortoise;
and skillfully he stretched oxhide round the shell
50 and on it he fixed two arms joined by a crosspiece
from which he stretched seven harmonious strings of
    sheep-gut.
And when it was finished, he held up the lovely toy
and with the plectron struck it tunefully, and under his
    hand
the lyre rang awesome. The god sang to it beautifully,

55 as on the lyre he tried improvisations, such as young men
      do
    at the time of feasts when they taunt and mock each other.
    He sang of Zeus Kronides and fair-sandaled Maia,
    and how they once dallied in the bond of love,
    recounting in detail his own glorious birth.
60 He also praised the handmaidens, and the splendid home
      of the nymph
    and the tripods throughout her dwelling, and the
      imperishable cauldrons.
    That is what he sang, but other matters engaged his mind.
    He carried the hollow lyre and laid it down

. . . .

    Then he easily soothed the far-shooting
    son of glorious Leto, exactly as he wished,
    mightier though Apollon was. Upon his left arm he took
    the lyre and with the plectron struck it tunefully, and
      under his hand
420 it resounded awesomely. And Phoibos Apollon laughed
    for joy as the lovely sound of the divine music
    went through to his heart and sweet longing seized him
    as he listened attentively. Playing sweetly on the lyre,
    the son of Maia boldly stood to the left
425 of Phoibos Apollon and to the clear-sounding lyre
    he sang as one sings preludes. His voice came out lovely,
    and he sang of the immortal gods and of black earth,
    how they came to be, and how each received his lot.
    Of the gods with his song he first honored Mnemosyne,
430 mother of the Muses, for the son of Maia fell to her lot.
    And the glorious son of Zeus honored the immortals
    according to age, and as each one had been born,
    singing of everything in due order as he played the lyre on
      his arm.
    But a stubborn longing seized Apollon's heart in his breast,
435 and he spoke to him and addressed him with winged
      words:
    "Scheming cattle-slayer, industrious comrade of the feast,

your performance is worth fifty cows;
I think we will settle our accounts at peace.
But come now, tell me this, inventive son of Maia:
440   Have these wondrous deeds followed you from birth,
or has some mortal man or deathless god
given you this glorious gift and taught you divine song?
Wondrous is this new-uttered sound I hear,
and such as I think no man or deathless god
445   dwelling on Olympos has ever yet learned,
except for you, O robber, son of Zeus and Maia.
What skill is this? What music for inescapable cares?
What virtuosity? For surely here are three things to take
all at once: good cheer, love, and sweet sleep.
450   I, too, am a follower of the Olympian Muses,
who cherish dance and the glorious field of song
and the festive chant and the lovely resonance of flutes.
But no display of skill by young men at feast
has ever touched my heart in this manner.
455   Son of Zeus, I marvel at your playing the lyre so
     charmingly.
Now, though you are little, since your ideas are
     remarkable,
sit down, friend, and have regard for the words of your
     elders.
There will indeed be renown for you among the immortals,
for you and your mother. I will speak concretely:
460   Yes, by the cornel spear, I shall truly make you
a glorious and thriving leader among the immortals,
and I shall give you splendid gifts without deception to the
     end."
And Hermes replied to him with calculated words:
"You question me carefully, Far-Shooter, and I
465   do not begrudge your becoming master of my skill.
You shall know it today. And I want to be gentle to you
in my words of advice—your mind knows all things well.
For, noble and mighty as you are, O son of Zeus, your seat
is first among the immortals, and wise Zeus loves you,

470 by every sacred right, and has granted you splendid gifts.
     And they say, O Far-Shooter, that from Zeus and his divine
       voice
     you learn the honors, the prophet's skills, and all god-
       given revelations.
     I myself have learned that you have all these in abundance.
     You may choose to learn whatever you desire,
475 but since your heart is so eager to play the lyre,
     sing and play the lyre and minister to gay festivities,
     receiving this skill from me and, friend, grant me glory.
     Sing well with this clear-voiced mistress in your arms,
     since you have the gift of beautiful and proper speech.
480 From now on in carefree spirit bring it to the well-
       provided feast,
     the lovely dance, and the revel where men vie for glory,
     as a fountain of good cheer day and night. Whoever
     with skill and wisdom expertly asks, to him
     it will speak and teach him all manner of things
485 joyful to the mind, being played with a gentle touch,
     for it shuns toilsome practice. But if anyone should
     in ignorance question it at first with rudeness,
     to him in vain it will chatter high-flown gibberish forever.
     You may choose to learn whatever you desire;
490 and I will make a gift of it to you, glorious son of Zeus.
     For my part, O Far-Shooter, I will graze the roving cattle
     on the pastures of the mountain and the horse-nurturing
       plain,
     where the cows are mounted by the bulls to give birth
     to males and females at random. And though your mind
495 is set on profit, there is no need for you to rage with
      anger."
     With these words he offered him the lyre, and Phoibos
      Apollon took it,
     and put in Hermes' hand a shining whip,
     and commanded him to be a cowherd. The son of Maia
      accepted
     joyfully. And the glorious son of Leto, far-shooting

500 lord Apollon upon his left arm took the lyre
     and struck it tunefully with the plectron. It resounded
     awesomely under his hand, and the god sang to it
        beautifully.
     Then both of them turned the cows toward
     the divine meadow, and the beautiful children of Zeus
505 rushed to return to snowy Olympos,
     delighting in the lyre; and thus wise Zeus rejoiced
     and brought them together in friendship.

> "To Hermes," lines 1–63, 416–507, *The Homeric Hymns,*
> trans. Apostolos N. Athanassakis (Baltimore:
> Johns Hopkins University Press, 1976).

Pherecrates

In the *Cheiron* by the comic poet Pherecrates (fifth to fourth century B.C.), the female character Music accuses Melanippides, Cinesias, Phrynis, and Timotheus of introducing innovations in the composition of dithyrambs and citharodic nomoi. Music complains to Justice about all the abuses she has received, emphasizing especially the confusion of the harmoniae and the new techniques for tuning instruments (Phrynis's *strobilos* was probably a sort of *capotasto,* a device for changing the tuning of the cithara).[1] In this passage the use of erotic language applied to the musical sphere produces a series of *doubles entendres,* since the innovations of the dithyrambic poets are described as acts of sexual violence which music is made to suffer. The "twelve strings" mentioned here in connection with Melanippides and Timotheus could perhaps be identified with the sounds (e.g., mi, ♯mi, fa, ♯fa, sol, la, ti, ♯ti, do, ♯do, re, mi) which within an octave (two tetrachords mi–la; ti–mi with tone of disjunction la–ti) made it possible for melodies to be executed in the three genera—diatonic, chromatic, and enharmonic.

Then gladly will I speak; you in the hearing
Will find your pleasure, in the telling I.

My woes began with Melanippides.
He was the first who took and lowered me,
Making me looser with his dozen strings.
Yet after all I found him passable
Compared with what I suffer now.
But the Athenian, curst Cinesias,
Producing off-key shifts in every movement
Has so undone me that his dithyrambs
Like objects mirrored in a polished shield
Show his dexterity to be left-handed.
Yet still and all I could put up with him.
But Phrynis had a screwbolt all his own
And bent and twisted me to my perdition;
His pentachords would play a dozen keys.
Yet him too in the end I could accept,
For he recovered later when he slipped.
But Oh! my dear, Timotheüs is murder,
Mayhem and outrage!—And who is the man?
—A redhead from Miletus. He's been worse
Than all the other fellows put together;
His notes crawl up and down the scale like ants,
And when he finds me on a walk alone
He tears and breaks me with his dozen strings.

> Pherecrates fr. 157; 145 Kock = Ps.-Plut. *De mus.* 1141d–f,
> trans. B. Einarson and P. H. de Lacy (Cambridge:
> Loeb Classical Library, 1967).

Plato

In the *Republic* and the *Laws*, Plato examines musical phenomena especially from the viewpoint of their influence on the character of the young and on the behavior of citizens in general. The dominant theme is the rejection of the "mimetic" music of the dithyrambic poets and Timotheus, and the regret for the musical forms of the previous century, which used to obey rigorous norms of composition and respect the ethical and esthetic canons prescribed by tradition. The first of the three passages that follow (*Rep.* 3.398c–399d) is based on the assumptions established by Damon's doctrine: those harmoniae—and their accompanying instruments—which trouble the souls of the citizens cannot be admitted into the State. The second passage (*Laws* 3.700a–701b) describes the nature of musical performance before and after the reform of Timotheus, with critical observations on the behavior of the audience at the theater. Finally (*Laws* 7.812b–813a), Plato states the norms which must regulate the teaching of instrumental music.

THE HARMONIAI

There remains the question of style in song and poetry set to music. It must be easy now for anyone to discover the rules we must make as to their character, if we are to be consistent.

Glaucon laughed. I am afraid 'anyone' does not include me, Socrates. At the moment I cannot quite see what the rules should be, though I have my suspicions.

You can see this much at any rate, that song consists of three elements: words, musical mode, and rhythm.

Yes.

And so far as the words go, it will make no difference whether they are set to music or not; in either case they must conform to the rules we have already made for the content and form of literature.

True.

And the musical mode and the rhythm should fit the words?

Of course.

And we said that we did not want dirges and laments. Which are the modes that express sorrow? Tell me; you are musical.

Modes like the Mixed Lydian and Hyperlydian.

Then we may discard those; men, and even women of good standing, will have no use for them.

Certainly.

Again, drunkenness, effeminacy, and inactivity are most unsuitable in Guardians. Which are the modes expressing softness and the ones used at drinking-parties?

129

There are the Ionian and certain Lydian modes which are called 'slack.'

You will not use them in the training of your warriors?

Certainly not. You seem to have the Dorian and the Phrygian left.

I am not an expert in the modes, I said; but leave me one which will fittingly represent the tones and accents of a brave man in warlike action or in any hard and dangerous task, who, in the hour of defeat or when facing wounds and death, will meet every blow of fortune with steadfast endurance. We shall need another to express peaceful action under no stress of hard necessity; as when a man is using persuasion or entreaty, praying to the gods or instructing and admonishing his neighbour, or again submitting himself to the instruction and persuasion of others; a man who is not overbearing when any such action has proved successful, but behaves always with wise restraint and is content with the outcome. These two modes you must leave: the two which will best express the accents of courage in the face of stern necessity and misfortune, and of temperance in prosperity won by peaceful pursuits.

The modes you want, he replied, are just the two I mentioned.

Our songs and airs, then, will not need instruments of large compass capable of modulation into all the modes, and we shall not maintain craftsmen to make them, in particular the flute, which has the largest compass of all. That leaves the lyre and the cithara for use in the town; and in the country the herdsmen may have some sort of pipe.

That seems to be the conclusion.

The Republic of Plato, 3.398c–399d, trans. F. M. Cornford
(Oxford, 1941).

MUSICAL GENRES BEFORE AND AFTER
THE REFORM OF TIMOTHEUS

Ath. I will. Under the ancient laws, my friends, the people was not as now the master, but rather the willing servant of the laws.

Meg. What laws do you mean?

Ath. In the first place, let us speak of the laws about music; that is to say, such music as then existed; in order that we may trace the growth of the excess of freedom from the beginning; for music was early divided among us into certain kinds and manners. One sort consisted of prayers to the Gods, which were called hymns; and there was another and opposite sort called lamentations, and another termed paeans, and another called dithyrambs; of which latter the subject, if I am not mistaken, was the birth of Dionysus. And they used the actual word 'laws,' or *nomoi,* meaning 'song,' only adding such and such an instrument, of the harp, for example, when they wanted to denote a particular strain. All these and others were duly distinguished, nor were they allowed to intermingle one sort of music with another. And the authority which determined and gave judgment, and punished the disobedient, was not expressed in a hiss, nor in the most unmusical 'sweet voices' of the multitude, as in our days; nor in applause and clappings of the hands. But the directors of public instruction insisted that the spectators should listen in silence to the end; and boys and their tutors, and the multitude in general, were kept quiet by the touch of the wand. Such was the good order which the multitude were willing to observe; they would not have dared to give judgment by noisy cries. And then, as time went on, the poets themselves introduced the reign of ignorance and misrule. They were men of genius, but they had no knowledge of what is just and lawful in music; raging like Bacchanals and possessed with inordinate delights—mingling lamentations with hymns, and paeans with dithyrambs; imitating the sounds of the flute on the lyre, and making one general confusion; ignorantly affirming that music has no truth, and, whether good or bad, can only be judged of rightly by the pleasure of the hearer. And by composing such licentious poems, and adding to them words as licentious, they have inspired the multitude with lawlessness and boldness, and made them fancy that they can judge for themselves about melody and song. And in this way the theatres from being mute have become vocal, as though they had understanding of good and bad in music and poetry; and instead of an aristocracy, an evil sort of theatrocracy

131

has grown up. For if the democracy which judged had only consisted of freemen, there would have been no fatal harm done; but in music there first arose the universal conceit of omniscience and general lawlessness;—freedom came following afterwards, and men, fancying that they knew what they did not know, had no longer any fear, and the absence of fear begets shamelessness. For what is shamelessness but the insolent refusal to regard the opinion of the better by reason of an over-daring sort of liberty?

Meg. Very true.

> *Laws,* 3.700a–701b, in *The Dialogues of Plato,*
> trans. B. Jowett (Oxford, 1875).

THE TEACHING OF MUSIC

Ath. And now that we have done with the teacher of letters, the teacher of the lyre has to receive orders from us.

Cle. Certainly.

Ath. I think that we have only to recollect our previous discussions, and we shall be able to give suitable regulations touching all this part of instruction and education to the teachers of the lyre.

Cle. To what do you refer?

Ath. We were saying, if I remember rightly, that the sixty years' old choristers of Dionysus were to be specially quick in their perceptions of rhythm and musical composition, that they might be able to distinguish good and bad imitation, or in other words, the imitation of the good or bad soul when under the influence of passion, rejecting the one and displaying the other in hymns and songs, charming the souls of youth, and inviting them to follow and attain virtue by the way of imitation.

Cle. Very true.

Ath. And with this view the teacher and the learner ought to use the sounds of the lyre because its notes are pure, the player who teaches and his pupil giving note for note in unison; but complexity, and variation of notes, when the strings give one sound and the poet or composer of the melody gives another; also when they make concords and harmonies in which lesser and greater intervals, slow and quick, or high and low notes, are combined; or, again, when they make complex variations of rhythms, which they adapt to the notes of the lyre—all that sort of thing is not suited to those who have to acquire a speedy and useful knowledge of music in three years; for opposite principles are confusing, and create a difficulty in learning, and our young men should learn quickly, and their mere necessary acquirements are not few or trifling, as will be shown in due course. Let our educator attend to the principles concerning music which we are laying down. As to the songs and words themselves which the masters of choruses are to teach and the character of them, they have been already described by us, and are the same which we said were to be consecrated as may suit the several feasts, and so furnish an innocent and useful amusement to cities.

Cle. That, again, is true.

Ath. Then let the musical president who has been elected receive these rules from us as the very truth; and may he prosper in his office!

> *Laws,* 7.812b–813a, in *The Dialogues of Plato,* trans. B. Jowett
> (Oxford, 1875).

Anonymous Speech on Music (Fourth Century B.C.?)

Preserved in a papyrus (*PHibeh* 1.13) is the beginning of a speech on music whose anonymous author probably lived in the fourth century.[2] The document contests the validity of the doctrine which attributes an ethical value to melody. In particular, it criticizes the view that the *gene* (diatonic, enharmonic, and chromatic) have the power to influence the souls of the listeners—a point which implies that the genus was regarded as an essential element for defining the harmonia and its moral character. The fragment represents the most ancient testimony of the activity of students of musical phenomena who did not align themselves with the Pythagorean-Damonic school.

It has often occurred to me to be surprised, men [of Greece], at the way certain people construct demonstrations not belonging to [their own areas of expertise], without your noticing. For they say that they are 'harmonicists'; and they pick out [various songs] and judge them against one another, condemning some, quite at random, and unsystematically extolling others. Again, they say that it is not their business to think about instrumentalists and singers: these matters, they say, they leave to others, while their own special province is the theoretical branch. Yet they actually display an immoderate enthusiasm for the things they leave to others, while improvising haphazardly in the areas where they say their strength lies.

They also say that some melodies make people self-disciplined, others prudent, others just, others brave, and others cowardly, not understanding that the chromatic cannot make cowards nor the enharmonic make brave men of those who employ it. For who does not know that the Aetolians and Dolopes and all those at Thermopylae, though they employ diatonic music, are braver than singers in tragedy, who have [always] been accustomed to singing in the enharmonic? Hence the chromatic does not make people cowardly, nor does the enharmonic make them brave.

These people have the effrontery to waste [their entire life] on strings. They play on strings [much worse than real instrumentalists], they sing much worse than real singers, and in their critical comparisons they do everything worse than any orator one might come across.

As to what is called 'harmonics', with which they say they have a special familiarity, they have nothing articulate to say, but are carried away with enthusiasm: and they beat the rhythm all wrong, on the wooden bench where they sit, [simultaneously] with the sounds of the *psaltērion*.

They do not even hesitate to state openly that some melodies will have a feature [peculiarly characteristic] of laurel, others of ivy.

PHibeh 1.13, *Greek Musical Writings*, I, ed. Andrew Barker (Cambridge, 1984).

Aristotle

The last book of Aristotle's *Politics* is devoted entirely to the problems of education, and of musical education in particular. After considering the reasons why music should figure in the curriculum of study of boys (*Pol.* 8.1337b23–1337b32; 1339a14–1340a14), Aristotle emphasizes its ethical value, greater than that of any other form of artistic expression (1340a14–1340b19). The author then confronts the problem of musical education, whose aim should not be to prepare the young for a professional activity unworthy of free men, but simply to provide them with the necessary competence for enjoying beautiful songs and rhythms (1340b20–1341b18). Aristotle here moves away from Platonic thought as he recognizes the moral usefulness of all forms of musical compositions according to the different requirements of the listeners.

MUSICAL EDUCATION

The customary branches of education are in number four; they are—(1) reading and writing, (2) gymnastic exercises, (3) music, to which is sometimes added (4) drawing. Of these, reading and writing and drawing are regarded as useful for the purposes of life in a variety of ways, and gymnastic exercises are thought to infuse courage. Concerning music a doubt may be raised—in our own day most men cultivate it for the sake of pleasure, but originally it was included in education, because nature herself, as has been often said, requires that we should be able, not only to work well, but to use leisure well; for, as I must repeat once and again, the first principle of all action is leisure. . . . It is not easy to determine the nature of music, or why any one should have a knowledge of it. Shall we say, for the sake of amusement and relaxation, like sleep or drinking, which are not good in themselves, but are pleasant, and at the same time "make care to cease," as Euripides says? And therefore men rank them with music, and make use of all three— sleep, drinking, music—to which some add dancing. Or shall we argue that music conduces to virtue, on the ground that it can form our minds and habituate us to true pleasures as our bodies are made by gymnastic to be of a certain character? Or shall we say that it contributes to the enjoyment of leisure and mental cultivation, which is a third alternative? Now obviously youth are not to be instructed with a view to their amusement, for learning is no pleasure, but is accompanied with pain. Neither is intellectual enjoyment suitable to boys of that age, for it is the end, and that which is imperfect cannot attain the perfect or end. But perhaps it may be said that boys learn music for the sake of the amusement which they will have when they are grown up. If so, why should they learn themselves, and not, like the Persian and Median kings, enjoy the pleasure and instruction which is derived from hearing others? (for surely skilled persons who have made music the business and profession of their lives will be better performers than those who practise only to learn). If they must learn music, on the same principle they should learn cookery, which is absurd. And even granting that music may form the character, the objection still holds: why should we learn ourselves? Why cannot we attain true pleasure and form a correct judgment from hearing others, like the Lacedaemonians?—for they, without learning music, nevertheless can correctly judge, as they say, of good and bad melodies. Or again, if music should be used to promote cheerfulness and refined intellectual enjoyment, the objection still remains—why should we learn ourselves instead of enjoying the performances of others? We may illustrate what we are saying by our conception of the Gods; for in the poets Zeus does not himself sing or play on the lyre. Nay, we call professional performers vulgar; no freeman would play or sing unless he were intoxicated or in jest. But these matters may be left for the present.

The first question is whether music is or is not to be a part of education. Of the three things mentioned in our discussion, which is it?—Education or amusement or intellectual enjoyment, for it may be reckoned under all three, and seems to share in the nature of all of them. Amusement is for the sake of relaxation, and relaxation is of necessity sweet, for it is the remedy of pain caused by toil, and intellectual enjoyment is universally acknowledged to contain an element not only of the noble but of the pleasant, for happiness is made up of both. All men agree that music is one of the pleasantest things, with or without song; as Musaeus says,

Song is to mortals of all things the sweetest.

Hence and with good reason it is introduced into social gatherings and entertainments, because it makes the hearts of men glad: so that on this ground alone we may assume that the young ought to be trained in it. For innocent pleasures are not only in harmony with the perfect end of life, but they also provide relaxation. And whereas men rarely attain the end, but often rest by the way and amuse themselves, not only with a view to some good, but also for the pleasure's sake, it may be well for them at times to find a refreshment in music. It sometimes happens that men make amusement the end, for the end probably contains some element of pleasure, though not any ordinary or lower pleasure; but they mistake the lower for the higher, and in seeking for the one find the other, since every pleasure has a likeness to the end of action. For the end is not eligible, nor do the pleasures which we have described exist, for the sake of any future good but of the past, that is to say, they are the alleviation of past toils and pains. And we may infer this to be the reason why men seek happiness from common pleasures. But music is pursued, not only as an alleviation of past toil, but also as providing recreation. And who can say whether, having this use, it may not also have a nobler one? In addition to this common pleasure, felt and shared in by all (for the pleasure given by music is natural, and therefore adapted to all ages and characters), may it not have also some influence over the character and the soul? It must have such an influence if characters are affected by it. And that they are so affected is proved by the power which the songs of Olympus and of many others exercise; for beyond question they inspire enthusiasm, and enthusiasm is an emotion of the ethical part of the soul. Besides, when men hear imitations, even unaccompanied by melody or rhythm, their feelings move in sympathy.

The Politics of Aristotle, 8.1337b23–32; 1339a14–1340a14, trans. B. Jowett (Oxford, 1885).

INFLUENCE OF MUSIC ON CHARACTER

Since then music is a pleasure, and virtue consists in rejoicing and loving and hating aright, there is clearly nothing which we are so much concerned to acquire and to cultivate as the power of forming right judgments, and of taking delight in good dispositions and noble actions. Rhythm and melody supply imitations of anger and gentleness, and also of courage and temperance and of virtues and vices in general, which hardly fall short of the actual affections, as we know from our own experience, for in listening to such strains our souls undergo a change. The habit of feeling pleasure or pain at mere representations is not far removed from the same feeling about realities; for example, if any one delights in the sight of a statue for its beauty only, it necessarily follows that the sight of the original will be pleasant to him. No other sense, such as taste or touch, has any resemblance to moral qualities; in sight only there is a little. . . . On the other hand, even in mere melodies there is an imitation of character, for the musical modes differ essentially from one another, and those who hear them are differently affected by each. Some of them make men sad and grave, like the so-called Mixolydian, others enfeeble the mind, like the relaxed harmonies, others, again, produce a moderate and settled temper, which appears to be the peculiar effect of the Dorian; the Phrygian inspires enthusiasm. The whole subject has been well treated by philosophical writers on this branch of education, and they confirm their arguments by facts. The same principles apply to rhythms: some have a character of rest, others of motion, and of these latter again, some have a more vulgar, others a nobler movement. Enough has been said to show that music has a power of forming the character, and should therefore be introduced into the education of the young. The study is suited to the stage of youth, for young persons will not, if they can help, endure anything which is not sweetened by pleasure, and music has a natural sweetness. There seems to be in us a sort of affinity to harmonies and rhythms, which makes some philosophers say that the soul is a harmony, others, that she possesses harmony.

The Politics of Aristotle, 1340a14–b19, trans. B. Jowett
(Oxford, 1885).

HOW THE YOUNG SHOULD LEARN MUSIC.
PROFESSIONALISM AND AMATEURISM.

And now we have to determine the question which has been already raised, whether children should be themselves taught to sing and play or not. Clearly there is a considerable difference made in the character by the actual practice of the art. It is difficult, if not impossible, for those who do not perform to be good judges of the performance of others. Besides, children should have something to do, and the rattle of Archytas, which people give to their children in order to amuse them and prevent them from breaking anything in the house, was a capital invention, for a young thing cannot be quiet. The rattle is a toy suited to the infant mind, and [musical] education is a rattle or toy for children of a larger growth. We conclude then that they should be taught music in such a way as to become not only critics but performers.

The question what is or is not suitable for different ages may be easily answered; nor is there any difficulty in meeting the objection of those who say that the study of music is vulgar. We reply (1) in the first place, that they who are to be judges must also be performers, and that they should begin to practise early, although when they are older they may be spared the execution; they must have learned to appreciate what is good and to delight in it, thanks to the knowledge which they acquired in their youth. As to (2) the vulgarizing effect which music is supposed to exercise, this is a question [of degree], which we shall have no difficulty in determining, when we have considered to what extent freemen who are being trained to political virtue should pursue the art, what melodies and what rhythms they should be allowed to use, and what instruments should be employed in teaching them to play, for even the instrument makes a difference. The answer to the objection turns upon these distinctions; for it is quite possible that certain methods of teaching and learning music do really have a degrading effect. It is evident then that the learning of music ought not to impede the business of riper years, or to degrade the body or render it unfit for civil or military duties, whether for the early practice or for the later study of them.

The right measure will be attained if students of music stop short of the arts which are practised in professional contexts, and do not seek to acquire those fantastic marvels of execution which are now the fashion in such contests, and from these have passed into education. Let the young pursue their studies until they are able to feel delight in noble melodies and rhythms, and not merely in that common part of music in which every slave or child and even some animals find pleasure.

From these principles we may also infer what instruments should be used. The flute, or any other instrument which requires great skill, as for example the harp, ought not to be admitted into education, but only such as will make intelligent students of music or of the other parts of education. Besides, the flute is not an instrument which has a good moral effect; it is too exciting. The proper time for using it is when the performance aims not at instruction, but at the relief of the passions. And there is a further objection; the impediment which the flute presents to the use of the voice detracts from its educational value. The ancients therefore were right in forbidding the flute to youths and freemen, although they had once allowed it. For when their wealth gave them greater leisure, and they had loftier notions of excellence, being also elated with their success, both before and after the Persian War, with more zeal than discernment they pursued every kind of knowledge, and so they introduced the flute into education. At Lacedaemon there was a Choragus who led the Chorus with a flute, and at Athens the instrument became so popular that most freemen could play upon it. The popularity is shown by the tablet which Thrasippus dedicated when he furnished the Chorus to Ecphantides. Later experience enabled men to judge what was or was not really conducive to virtue, and they rejected both the flute and several other old-fashioned instruments, such as the Lydian harp, the many-stringed lyre, the heptagon, triangle, sambyke, and the like—which are intended only to give pleasure to the hearer, and require extraordinary skill of hand. There is a meaning also in the myth of the ancients, which tells how Athene invented the flute and then threw it away. It was not a bad idea of theirs, that the Goddess disliked the instrument because it made the face ugly;

but with still more reason may we say that she rejected it because the acquirement of flute-playing contributes nothing to the mind, since to Athene we ascribe both knowledge and art.

Thus then we reject the professional instruments and also the professional mode of education in music—and by professional we mean that which is adopted in contests, for in this the performer practises the art, not for the sake of his own improvement, but in order to give pleasure, and that of a vulgar sort, to his hearers. For this reason the execution of such music is not the part of a freeman but of a paid performer, and the result is that the performers are vulgarized, for the end at which they aim is bad. The vulgarity of the spectator tends to lower the character of the music and therefore of the performers; they look to him—he makes them what they are, and fashions even their bodies by the movements which he expects them to exhibit.

The Politics of Aristotle, 8.1340b20–1341b18, trans. B. Jowett (Oxford, 1885).

HARMONIAE AND RHYTHMS

We have also to consider rhythms and harmonies. Shall we use them all in education or make a distinction? and shall the distinction be that which is made by those who are engaged in education, or shall it be some other? For we see that music is produced by melody and rhythm, and we ought to know what influence these have respectively on education, and whether we should prefer excellence in melody or excellence in rhythm. But as the subject has been very well treated by many musicians of the present day, and also by philosophers who have had considerable experience of musical education, to these we would refer the more exact student of the subject; we shall only speak of it now after the manner of the legislator, having regard to general principles.

We accept the division of melodies proposed by certain philosophers into ethical melodies, melodies of action, and passionate or inspiring melodies, each having, as they say, a mode or harmony corresponding to it. But we maintain further that music should be studied, not for the sake of one, but of many benefits, that is to say, with a view to (1) education, (2) purification (the word 'purification' we use at present without explanation, but when hereafter we speak of poetry, we will treat the subject with more precision); music may also serve (3) for intellectual enjoyment, for relaxation and for recreation after exertion. It is clear, therefore, that all the harmonies must be employed by us, but not all of them in the same manner. In education ethical melodies are to be preferred, but we may listen to the melodies of action and passion when they are performed by others. For feelings such as pity and fear, or, again, enthusiasm, exist very strongly in some souls, and have more or less influence over all. Some persons fall into a religious frenzy, whom we see disenthralled by the use of mystic melodies, which bring healing and purification to the soul. Those who are influenced by pity or fear and every emotional nature have a like experience, others in their degree are stirred by something which specially affects them, and all are in a manner purified and their souls lightened and delighted. The melodies of purification likewise give an innocent pleasure to mankind. Such are the harmonies and the melodies in which those who perform music at the theatre should be invited to compete. But since the spectators are of two kinds—the one free and educated, and the other a vulgar crowd composed of mechanics, labourers, and the like—there ought to be contests and exhibitions instituted for the relaxation of the second class also. And the melodies will correspond to their minds; for as their minds are perverted from the natural state, so there are exaggerated and corrupted harmonies which are in like manner a perversion. A man receives pleasure from what is natural to him, and therefore professional musicians may be allowed to practise this lower sort of music before an audience of a lower type. But, for the purposes of education, as I have already said, those modes and melodies should be employed which are ethical, such as the Dorian; though we may include any others which are approved by philosophers who have had a musical education. The Socrates of the *Republic* is wrong in retaining only the Phrygian mode along with the Dorian, and the more so because he rejects the flute; for the Phrygian is to the modes what the flute is to musical instruments—both of them are exciting and emotional. Poetry proves this, for Bacchic frenzy and all similar emotions are most suitably expressed by the flute, and are better set to the Phrygian than to any other harmony. The dithyramb, for example, is acknowledged to be Phrygian, a fact of which the connoisseurs of music offer many proofs, saying, among other things, that Philoxenus, having attempted to compose his "Tales" as a dithyramb in the Dorian mode, found it impossible, and fell back into the more appropriate Phrygian. All men agree that the Dorian music is the gravest and manliest. And whereas we say that the extremes should be avoided and the mean followed, and whereas the Dorian is a mean between the other harmonies [the Phrygian and the Lydian], it is evident that our youth should be taught the Dorian music.

Two principles have to be kept in view, what is possible, what is becoming: at these every man ought to aim. But even these are relative to age; the old, who have lost their powers, cannot very well sing the severe melodies, and nature herself seems to suggest that their songs should be of the more relaxed kind. Wherefore the musicians likewise blame Socrates, and with justice, for rejecting the relaxed harmonies in education under the idea that they are intoxicating, not in the ordinary sense of intoxication (for wine rather tends to excite men), but because they have no strength in them. And so with a view to a time of life when men begin to grow old, they ought to practise the gentler harmonies and melodies as well as the others. And if there be any harmony, such as the Lydian above all others appears to be, which is suited to children of tender age, and possesses the elements both of order and of education, clearly [we ought to use it, for] education should be based upon three principles—the mean, the possible, the becoming, these three.

The Politics of Aristotle, 8.1341b19–1342b34, trans. B. Jowett
(Oxford, 1885).

Pseudo-Aristotle, Musical Problems

The anonymous author of the *Musical Problems* attributed to Aristotle—certainly a Peripatetic who closely follows the master—confronts the question of why music and song give pleasure to the listener. His answer conforms to the opinions which Aristotle expresses on the subject in the last book of the *Politics* (see above). In particular, the author emphasizes the idea that order, innate in human nature, is also the essential element of rhythm and melody. Music consists in the mixture of opposites which bear a determined relation to one another. This fact enhances the power of music to give pleasure because what is mixed is more pleasurable than what is not.

Why does everyone enjoy rhythm and tune, and in general all consonances? Is it because we naturally enjoy natural movements? This is proved by the fact that newly born infants enjoy such. We enjoy different types of song for their moral character, but we enjoy rhythm because it has a recognized and orderly numerical arrangement and carries us along in an orderly fashion; for orderly movement is naturally more akin to us than one without order, so that such rhythm is more in accordance with nature. Here is a proof of this: if we take our exercise and eat and drink in an orderly fashion we preserve and improve our nature and our strength, but by a disorderly method we ruin and spoil it; for bodily diseases are unnatural disturbances of order. But we enjoy harmony, because it is a mingling of opposites which bear a relation to each other. Now a relation implies an ordered arrangement, which is naturally pleasant. But everything mixed is more pleasant than unmixed, especially if in the sensible world the relation existing in the harmony has the power of the two extremes in equal balance.

Problems, 1:19.38, trans. W. S. Hett (Cambridge: Loeb Classical Library, 1936).

Aristoxenus

In the introductory chapters of the second book of his *Harmonic Elements,* where he defines the purpose and method of his inquiry, Aristoxenus takes a position against the mutually opposite doctrines of those who, following Damon, consider harmonics (the science of intervals) as the basis of moral education and of those who deny to this discipline any ethical and pedagogical value. Aristoxenus also rejects the method of the Pythagoreans, who disregard sensible data and found their theory only on abstract numerical ratios. On the other hand, he also criticizes the *modus operandi* of those who attribute absolute value to their own subjective perceptions and limit themselves to recording musical phenomena empirically, without even attempting to explain in rational terms how they relate to one another.

Aristoxenus's position is balanced between these various contrasting tendencies. Harmonics is not the fundamental science for the formation of character, but neither is it an insignificant and negligible part of education; it represents an essential part of musical theory, like rhythmics, metrics, and organics. It is rather to music as a whole that we should attribute an important ethical and pedagogical power on the audience. Thus, the study of intervals cannot consist merely in defining mathematically the numerical ratios between different sounds, nor can it stop at the subjective and acritical observation of consonances and dissonances. Aristoxenus's inquiry is based on the data of sense perception, but he then proceeds to analyze these data rationally and to integrate them in a coherent theoretical system.

It will be well perhaps to review in anticipation the course of our study; thus a foreknowledge of the road that we must travel will enable us to recognize each stage as we reach it, and so lighten the toil of the journey; nor shall we be harbouring unknown to ourselves a false conception of our subject. Such was the condition, as Aristotle used often to relate, of most of the audience that attended Plato's lectures on the Good. They came, he used to say, every one of them, in the conviction that they would get from the lectures some one or other of the things that the world calls good; riches or health, or strength, in fine, some extraordinary gift of fortune. But when they found that Plato's reasonings were of sciences and numbers, and geometry, and astronomy, and of good and unity as predicates of the finite, methinks their disenchantment was complete. The result was that some of them sneered at the thing, while others vilified it. Now to what was all this trouble due? To the fact that they had not wanted to inform themselves of the nature of the subject, but after the manner of the sect of word-catchers had flocked round open-mouthed, attracted by the mere title 'good' in itself.

But if a general exposition of the subject had been given in advance, the intending pupil would either have abandoned his intention or if he was pleased with the exposition, would have remained in the said conviction to the end. It was for these very reasons, as he told us, that Aristotle himself used to give his intending pupils a preparatory statement of the subject and method of his course of study. And we agree with him in thinking, as we said at the beginning, that such prior information is desirable. For mistakes are often made in both directions. Some consider Harmonic a sublime science, and expect a course of it to make them musicians; nay some even conceive it will exalt their moral nature. This mistake is due to their having run away with such phrases in our preamble as "we aim at the construction of every style of melody," and with our general statement "one class of musical art is hurtful to the moral character, another improves it"; while they missed completely our qualification of this statement, "in so far as musical art can improve the moral character." Then on the other hand there are persons who regard Harmonic as quite a thing of no importance, and actually prefer to remain totally unacquainted even with its nature and aim. Neither of these views is correct. On the one hand the science is no proper object of contempt to the man of intelligence—this we shall see as the discussion progresses; nor on the other hand has it the quality of all-sufficiency, as some imagine. To be a musician, as we are always insisting, implies much more than a knowledge of Harmonic, which is only one part of the musician's equipment, on the same level as the sciences of rhythm, of metre, of instruments.

We shall now proceed to the consideration of Harmonic and its parts. It is to be observed that in general the subject of our study is the question, In melody of every kind what are the natural laws according to which the voice in ascending or descending places the intervals? For we hold that the voice follows a natural law in its motion, and does not place the intervals at random. And of our answers we endeavour to supply proofs that will be in agreement with the phenomena—in this unlike our predecessors. For some of these introduced extraneous reasoning, and rejecting the senses as inaccurate fabricated rational principles, asserting that height and depth of pitch consist in certain numerical ratios and relative rates of vibration—a theory utterly extraneous to the subject and quite at variance with the phenomena; while others, dispensing with reason and demonstration, confined themselves to isolated dogmatic statements, not being successful either in their enumeration of the mere phenomena. It is our endeavour that the principles which we assume shall without exception be evident to those who understand music, and that we shall advance to our conclusions by strict demonstration.

Our subject-matter then being all melody, whether vocal or instrumental, our method rests in the last resort on an appeal to the two faculties of hearing and intellect. By the former we judge the magnitudes of the intervals, by the latter we contemplate the functions of the notes. We must therefore accustom ourselves to an accurate discrimination of particulars. It is usual in geometrical constructions to use such a phrase as "Let this be a straight line"; but one must not be content with such language of assumption in the case of intervals. The geometrician makes no use of his faculty of sense-perception. He does not in any degree train his sight to discriminate the straight line, the circle, or any other figure, such training belonging rather to the practice of the carpenter, the turner, or some other such handicraftsman. But for the student of musical science accuracy of sense-perception is a fundamental requirement. For if his sense-perception is deficient, it is impossible for him to deal successfully with those questions that lie outside the sphere of sense-perception altogether.

The Harmonics of Aristoxenus, 2.30–33, ed. and trans.
Henry S. Macran (Oxford, 1902).

Aulus Gellius

In this chapter of the *Attic Nights* Aulus Gellius (second century), referring to a passage of Thucydides (5.70), examines the genres of military music in use among the ancients as well as their effects on the minds of the listeners. Certain musical pieces are suitable by their nature and rhythm for encouraging the fighters to advance slowly and in compact order; others incite them to rush forward in disorderly fashion without maintaining the initial array.

Those who listen to a political speech are also affected by an appropriate musical accompaniment. Cicero reports that Gaius Gracchus used to speak in the Forum with a *fistula* player standing next to him (the *fistula* was a sort of recorder). Gellius explains that the sound of the instrument had only the purpose of recalling Gracchus to moderation in moments of excessive ardor, while Cicero maintains that the aulete was supposed both to excite the orator when his eloquence was lacking, and to calm him down when his speech was too violent. These opinions are not entirely plausible, however. The music of the aulete was certainly meant for the benefit of the audience, and served to increase the impact and persuasiveness of the words.

Thucydides, the most authoritative of Greek historians, tells us that the Lacedaemonians, greatest of warriors, made use in battle, not of signals by horns or trumpets, but of the music of pipes, certainly not in conformity with any religious usage or from any ceremonial reason, nor yet that their courage might be roused and stimulated, which is the purpose of horns and trumpets; but on the contrary that they might be calmer and advance in better order, because the effect of the flute-player's notes is to restrain impetuosity. So firmly were they convinced that in meeting the enemy and beginning battle nothing contributed more to valour and confidence than to be soothed by gentler sounds and keep their feelings under control. Accordingly, when the army was drawn up, and began to advance in battle-array against the foe, pipers stationed in the ranks began to play. Thereupon, by this quiet, pleasant, and even solemn prelude the fierce impetuosity of the soldiers was checked, in conformity with a kind of discipline of military music, so to speak, so that they might not rush forth in straggling disorder.

But I should like to quote the very words of that outstanding writer, which have greater distinction and credibility than my own: "And after this the attack began. The Argives and their allies rushed forward eagerly and in a rage, but the Lacedaemonians advanced slowly to the music of many flute-players stationed at regular intervals; this not for any religious reason, but in order that they might make the attack while marching together rhythmically, and that their ranks might not be broken, which commonly happens to great armies when they advance to the attack."

Tradition has it that the Cretans also commonly entered battle with the lyre playing before them and regulating their step. Furthermore, Alyattes, king of the land of Lydia, a man of barbaric manners and luxury, when he made war on the Milesians, as Herodotus tells us in his *History,* had in his army and his battle-array orchestras of pipe- and lyre-players, and even female flute-players, such as are the delight of wanton banqueters. Homer, however, says that the Achaeans entered battle, relying, not on the music of lyres and pipes, but on silent harmony and unanimity of spirit:

In silence came the Achaeans, breathing rage,
Resolved in mind on one another's aid.

What then is the meaning of that soul-stirring shout of the Roman soldiers which, as the annalists have told us, was regularly raised when charging the foe? Was that done contrary to so generally accepted a rule of old-time discipline? Or are a quiet advance and silence needful when an army is marching against an enemy that is far off and visible from a distance, but when they have almost come to blows, then must the foe, already at close quarters, be driven back by a violent assault and terrified by shouting?

But, look you, the Laconian pipe-playing reminds me also of that oratorical pipe, which they say was played for Gaius Gracchus when he addressed the people, and gave him the proper pitch. But it is not at all true, as is commonly stated, that a musician always stood behind him as he spoke, playing the pipe, and by varying the pitch now restrained and now animated his feelings and his delivery. For what could be more absurd than that a piper should play measures, notes, and a kind of series of changing melodies for Gracchus when addressing an assembly, as if for a dancing mountebank? But more reliable authorities declare that the musician took his place unobserved in the audience and at intervals sounded on a short pipe a deeper note, to restrain and calm the exuberant energy of the orator's delivery. And that in my opinion is the correct view, for it is unthinkable that Gracchus' well-known natural vehemence needed any incitement or impulse from without. Yet Marcus Cicero thinks that the piper was employed by Gracchus for both purposes, in order that with notes now soft, now shrill, he might animate his oratory when it was becoming weak and feeble, or check it when too violent and passionate. I quote Cicero's own words: "And so this same Gracchus, Catulus, as you may hear from your client Licinius, an educated man, who was at that time Gracchus' slave and amanuensis, used to have a skilful musician stand behind him in concealment when he addressed an audience, who could quickly breathe a note to arouse the speaker if languid, or recall him from undue vehemence."

Finally, Aristotle wrote in his volume of *Problems* that the custom of the Lacedaemonians which I have mentioned, of entering battle to the music of pipers, was adopted in order to make the fearlessness and ardour of the soldiers more evident and indubitable. "For," said he, "distrust and fear are not at all consistent with an advance of that kind, and such an intrepid and rhythmical advance cannot be made by the faint-hearted and despondent." I have added a few of Aristotle's own words on the subject: "Why, when on the point of encountering danger, did they advance to music of the pipe? In order to detect the cowards by their failure to keep time."

The Attic Nights of Aulus Gellius, 1.11, trans. R. C. Rolfe
(London and New York: Loeb Classical Library, 1927).

Notes

Chapter I Introduction

1. The texts containing musical notation are published in Egert Pöhlmann, *Denkmäler altgriechischer Musik* (Nuremberg, 1970). Five new
   papyri with musical notes were discovered after 1970: *PLeid.* inv. 510,
   and *POxy.* 3161, 3162, 3704, and 3705. See Chapter 6.

2. A rich musical iconography can be found in Max Wegner, *Das Musikleben der Griechen* (Berlin, 1949); Max Wegner, "Griechenland," *Musikgeschichte in Bildern* 2, no. 4 (Leipzig, 1963); and G. Fleischhauer,
   "Etrurien und Rom," *Musikgeschichte in Bildern* 2, no. 5 (Leipzig,
   1965).

3. On music in Homer, see Max Wegner, "Musik und Tanz," *Archaeo-
   logia Homerica* 3 U (Gottingen, 1968), and M. L. West, "The Singing of
   Homer," *Journal of Hellenic Studies* 101 (1981): 113–29.

4. On the composition, diffusion, and transmission of musical texts, see
   Egert Pöhlmann, *Griechische Musikfragmente* (Nuremberg, 1960); A.
   Bataille, "Remarques sur les deux notations mélodiques de l'ancienne
   musique grecque," *Recherche de Papyrologie* 1 (1961): 5–20; J. Chail
   ley, "Nouvelles remarques sur les deux notations musicales grecques,"
   Recherche de Papyrologie 4 (1967): 201–19; I. Marrou, "Meolographia,"
   Antiquité Classique 15 (1946): 289–96.

5. On the relationship in general between poetry and society in archaic
   Greece, see Bruno Gentili, *Poetry and Its Public in Ancient Greece*
   (Baltimore, 1988), trans. A. Thomas Cole; first published as *Poesia e
   pubblico nella Grecia antica* (Rome and Bari, 1984).

153

6. See Wegner, *Musikleben*, Fig. 16a.
7. Examples other than the one illustrated: a volute krater, München 3278 F; a *kylix*, Cambridge G73; a *hydria*, London E171. See Wegner, *Musikleben*, Figs. 22, 31b, and 13. Other examples are cited in Egert Pöhlmann, *Griechische Musikfragmente* (Nuremberg, 1960), 83–84.
8. On theatrical promptbooks, see Bruno Gentili, *Lo spettacolo nel mondo antico* (Rome and Bari, 1977).
9. Ibid., 9, 19 ff.

Chapter II Greek Music

1. On the relationship between poetry and music, see Bruno Gentili, *Metrica greca arcaica* (Messina and Florence, 1950), 30–50, and "La metrica greca oggi: Problemi e metodologie," *Problemi di Metrica Classica* (Genoa, 1978), 11–18.
2. The most recent editions of the *De musica* of Pseudo-Plutarch are the following: Plutarque, *De la Musique,* ed. and trans. F. Lasserre (Olten and Lausanne, 1954); "De musica," in *Plutarchi Moralia*, vol. 6, pt. 3, 3d ed. (Leipzig, 1966), ed. K. Ziegler.
3. On ancient citharody, see Bruno Gentili and P. Giannini, "Preistoria e formazione dell'esametro," *Quaderni Urbinati* 26 (1977): 7–51. Also C. O. Pavese, "Tipologia Metrica Greca," *Problemi di Metrica Classica* (Genoa, 1978), 49–74.
4. Bruno Gentili and P. Giannini, "Preistoria," p. 34.
5. On poetic genres, see C. O. Pavese, *Tradizione e generi poetici nella Grecia arcaica* (Rome, 1972).
6. On *nomos*, see H. Grieser, *Nomos: Ein Beitrag zur griechischen Musikgeschichte* (Heidelberg, 1937); H. Koller, "Das kitharodische Prooimion," *Philologus* 100 (1956): 159–206; and C. Calame, ed., *Alcman* (Rome, 1983).
7. On Spartan civilization and culture, see P. Ianni, *La cultura di Sparta arcaica,* 2 vols. (Rome, 1965–70).
8. Bruno Gentili, "Il *partenio* di Alcmane e l'amore omoerotico femminile nei tíasi spartani," *Quaderni Urbinati* 22 (1976): 59–67; Claude Calame, *Les choeurs de jeunes filles en Grèce archaïque* (Rome, 1977), 2:39 ff.
9. Bruno Gentili, "I frr. 39 e 40 P. di Alcmane e la poetica della mimesi nella cultura greca arcaica," *Studi in onore di V. de Falco* (Naples, 1971), 57–67.
10. Bruno Gentili, s.v. "Parakataloghe," *Enciclopedia dello spettacolo* 7 (Rome, 1960), cols. 1599–1601; F. Perusino, *Il tetrametro giambico catalettico nella commedia greca* (Rome, 1968), 20–28.
11. Gentili, "Il *partenio* di Alcmane," 59–60.

12. On the characteristics of archaic poetry, see Bruno Gentili "Lirica greca arcaica e tardo-arcaica," *Introduzione allo studio della cultura classica* 1 (Milan, 1972): 57–105; H. Koller, *Musik und Dichtung im alten Griechenland* (Bern, 1963); Claude Calame, ed., *Rito e poesia corale in Grecia: Guida storica e critica* (Rome and Bari, 1977); H. Thiemer, *Der Einfluss der Phryger auf die altgriechische Musik* (Bonn and Bad Godesberg, 1979); and M. L. West, "Music in Archaic Greece," *Actes du VIIIe Congrès de la F.I.E.C.* (Budapest, 1984).

13. On the subject of the dithyramb, see Arthur W. Pickard-Cambridge, *Dithyramb, Tragedy, and Comedy*, 2d ed. (Oxford, 1962); G. A. Privitera, *Dioniso in Omero e nella poesia greca arcaica* (Rome, 1970), 36–42; and G. A. Privitera, "Il ditirambo da canto cultuale a spettacolo musicale," *Cultura e Scuola* 43 (1972): 56–66.

14. On the concept of *harmonia*, see R. P. Winnington-Ingram, *Mode in Ancient Greek Music* (Cambridge, 1936; repr. Amsterdam, 1968); O. Gombosi, *Tonarten und Stimmungen der antiken Musik* (Copenhagen, 1939).

15. On Lasus, see G. A. Privitera, *Laso di Ermione nella cultura ateniese e nella tradizione storiografica* (Rome, 1965); G. F. Brussich, "Laso d' Ermione: Testimonianze e frammenti," *Quaderni Triestini per lo Studio della Lirica Corale Greca* 3 (1975–76): 83–135.

16. See Privitera, *Laso di Ermione*, 21.

17. On the Pythagoreans, see M. Timpanaro Cardini, ed., *Pitagorici: testimonianze e frammenti*, 3 vols. (Florence, 1958–64).

18. On choral lyric generally, see Gentili, "Lirica greca arcaica e tardo-arcaica," 57–105, and "Aspetti del rapporto poeta, committente, uditorio nella lirica corale greca," *Studi Urbinati* 39 (1965): 70–88. On Bacchylides specifically, see Bruno Gentili, *Bacchilide: Studi* (Urbino, 1958).

19. On Pindar, see G. Marzi, "Pindaro e la musica," *Vichiana* n.s. 1 (1972): 3–15, and Gilbert Highet, *The Classical Tradition* (New York, 1950), 222–24.

20. P. Bernardini, "Rassegna critica delle edizioni, traduzioni e studi pindarici dal 1958 at 1964 (1965)," *Quaderni Urbinati* 2 (1966): 155.

21. The testimony concerning Damon is collected in U. v. Wilamowitz-Moellendorff, *Griechische Verskunst* (Berlin, 1921), 61–66, and François Lasserre, ed., *De la musique*, by Plutarque (Olten and Lausanne, 1954), 74–79.

22. On musical *ethos*, see Edward A. Lippman, *Musical Thought in Ancient Greece* (New York, 1964); Warren D. Anderson, *Ethos and Education in Greek Music*, 2d ed. (Cambridge, 1968); and François Lasserre, "Mimesis et Mimique," *Dioniso* 41 (1967): 245–63.

23. On drama at Athens, see Arthur W. Pickard-Cambridge, *The Dramatic*

Tragic Theater (New York, 1971). On music in tragedy, see F. Marx, "Music in der griechischen Tragödie," *Reinisches Museum* 82 (1933): 230–46; V. Pappalardo, "Vicende della notazione musical nei testi drammatici greci," *Memorie Ist. Lombardo-Acc. Scienze e Lettere* 35 (1975): 355–413; and M. Pintacuda, *La musica nella tragedia greca* (Cefalù, 1978). See also L. Richter, "Instrumental Begleitung zur attischen Tragödie," *Altertum* 24 (1978): 150–59; L. Richter, "Die Musik der Griechischen Tragödie," *Die Griechische Tragödie in ihrer Gesellschaftlichen Funktion,* ed. by H. Kuck (Berlin, 1983), 115–39; J. Lohmann, "Die Geburt der Tragödie aus dem Geiste der Musik," *Arkiv für Musikwissenschaft* 37 (1980): 167–86; M. Pintacuda, *Interpretazioni musicali sul teatro de Aristofane* (Palermo, 1982); and J. H. Galy, "La musique dans la comédie grecque des V et IV s.," *Ann. Fac. Lett. Nice* 50 (1985): 77–94.

24. The fragments of the dithyrambic poets and the testimony regarding their lives are collected in C. del Grande, *Ditirambografi: Testimonianze e frammenti* (Naples, 1946). See also A. W. Pickard-Cambridge, *Dithyramb, Tragedy, and Comedy* (Oxford, 1927).

25. The papyrus of the *Persians* of Timotheus is published in U. v. Wilamowitz-Moellendorff, *Timotheus, die Perser* (Leipzig, 1903).

26. Giovanni Comotti, "L'endecacordo di Ione di Chio," *Quaderni Urbinati* 13 (1972): 54–61.

27. On the new dithyramb, see H. Schonewolf, *Der jungattische Dithyrambos* (Diss. Giessen, 1938), and D. Restani, "Il *Chirone* di Ferecrate e la 'nuova' musica greca," *Riv. Italiana di Musicologia* 18 (1983): 139–92.

28. On music in Plato and Aristotle, see E. Moutsopoulos, *La musique dans l'oeuvre de Platon* (Paris, 1959), and Lukas Richter, *Zur Wissenschaftlehre von der Musik bei Platon und Aristoteles* (Berlin, 1961). Also, H. Koller, "Musik bei Platon und die Pythagoreern," *Propyläen-Gesch. der Literatur* 1 (Berlin, 1981): 275–88, and Lukas Richter, "Die Stellung der Musik in der Aristotelischen Metaphysik," in *Aristoteles als Wissenschaftstheoriker,* ed. J. Irmscher and R. Mueller (Berlin, 1983), 46–49.

29. On music in Hellenistic theater, see G. M. Sifakis, *Studies in the History of Hellenistic Drama* (London, 1967), and Bruno Gentili, *Lo spettacolo nel mondo antico* (Rome and Bari, 1977).

30. M. Guarducci, "Poeti vaganti e conferenzieri dell'età ellenistica," *Atti R. Acc. Naz. Lincei, Classe di scienze morali, storiche e filologiche,* 6, vol. 2 (1927–29), 629–65.

31. Sifakis, *Studies in the History of Hellenistic Drama,* 63 ff.; Gentili, *Lo spettacolo nel mondo antico,* 4 ff.

32. Reprinted in Sources, below, p. 133.
33. On the theories of Aristoxenus, see Rudolf Westphal, *Aristoxenos von Tarent: Melik und Rythmik des klassischen Altertums* (Leipzig, 1883; repr. Hildesheim, 1965); L. Laloy, *Aristoxène de Tarente et la musique de l'antiquité* (Paris, 1904); R. P. Winnington-Ingram, "Aristoxenus and the Intervals of Music," *Classical Quarterly* 26 (1932): 195–208.
34. R. Schäfke, ed., *Von der Musik*, by Aristides Quintilianus (Berlin and Schoneberg, 1937), and L. Zanoncelli, "La filosofia musicale di Aristide Quintiliano," *Quaderni Urbinati* 24 (1977): 87–93.
35. Bruno Gentili, "La metrica greca oggi: Problemi e Metodologie," 18.
36. E. Fubini, *L'estetica musicale dal Settecento ad oggi*, 5th ed. (Turin, 1974), 15–59.
37. L. Zanoncelli, "La filosofia musicale di Aristide Quintiliano," *Quaderni Urbinati* 24 (1977): 52–72.

Chapter III Roman Music

1. E. La Rocca, "Note sulle importazioni greche in territorio laziale nell'VIII secolo a.C.," *La parola del passato* 177 (1977): 375–97.
2. On Roman music in general, see G. Wille, *Musica Romana* (Amsterdam, 1967), and his *Einführung in das Römisches Musikleben* (Darmstadt, 1977).
3. Bruno Gentili, *Lo spettacolo nel mondo antico*, 5, 19, 24–28 ff.; S. Eitrem, L. Amundsen, and R. P. Winnington-Ingram, "Fragments of Unknown Greek Tragic Texts with Musical Notation (*POsl.* 1413)," *Symbolae Osloenses* 31 (1955): 1–87.
4. On the rhythms of Plautus's comedy, see C. Questa, *Introduzione sulla metrica di Plauto* (Bologna, 1967).
5. See Cassiodorus, *Chronica a 639 ab U.c.*, and G. Rotondi, *Leges Publicae Populi Romani* (Milan, 1912; repr. Hildesheim, 1966), 320.
6. Wille, *Musica Romana*, 413–20.
7. On the different aspects of musical culture in the imperial age, see L. Friedlander, *Darstellungen aus der Sittengeschichte Roms*, 10th ed. (Leipzig, 1922; repr. Aalen, 1964), 2:112–47, 163–90; and E. J. Jory, "The Literary Evidence for the Beginning of Imperial Pantomime," *Bull. Institute of Classical Studies, Univ. London* 28 (1981): 147–61.
8. On the musical expressions of pagan and Christian cults, see J. Quastern, *Musik und Gesang in den Kulten der heidnischen Antike und christlichen Frühzeit* (Munich, 1930).
9. On ancient Christian music, see J. Chailley, *Histoire musicale du Moyen Age* (Paris, 1950), 1–40.
10. Egert Pöhlmann, *Denkmäler altgriechischer Musik* (Nuremberg, 1970), 106 ff.

Chapter IV Musical Instruments

1. Giovanni Comotti, "L'endecacordo di Ione di Chio," *Quaderni Urbinati* 13 (1972): 54–61.
2. Max Wegner, *Das Musikleben der Griechen* (Berlin, 1949), Figs. 14, 15a, and 15b.
3. Ibid., 46.
4. See Jean M. Davison, "Attic Geometric Workshops," *Yale Classical Studies* 15 (1961): 83 ff., Fig. 127. Also, A. Bélis, "A propos de la construction de la Lyre," *Bull. Corresp. Héll.* 109 (1985): 201–20.
5. M. L. West, "The Singing of Homer and the Modes of Early Greek Music," *Journal of Hellenic Studies* 101 (1981): 113–29.
6. Wegner, *Musikleben,* pp. 31, 206–8 (s.v. "Wiegen-Kithara").
7. Reinhard Herbig, "Griechische Harfen," *Mitteilung des deutschen Archäologischen Instituts: Athenische Abteilung,* 54 (1929): 164–93.
8. Giovanni Comotti, "Un' antica arpa, la *mágadis,* in un frammento di Teleste (fr. 808P.)," *Quaderni Urbinati* n.s. 15 [44] (1983): 57–71.
9. Herbig, "Griechische Harfen," Fig. 6.
10. Curt Sachs, *The History of Musical Instruments* (New York, 1940), 137.
11. See R. A. Higgins and R. P. Winnington-Ingram, "Lute-Players in Greek Art," *Journal of Hellenic Studies* 85 (1965): 62 ff.
12. Kathleen Schlesinger, *The Greek Aulos* (London, 1939).
13. Giovanni Comotti, "L'aulo *ghingras* in una scena menandrea del mosaico di Diocuride," *Quaderni Urbinati* 20 (1975): 215–23. See also A. Bélis, "Auloi grecs du Louvre," *Bull. Corresp. Héll.* 108 (1984): 111–22.
14. Max Wegner, *Musikgeschichte in Bilder,* vol. 2, *Griechenland* (Leipzig, 1963), 80–81.
15. Giovanni Comotti, "L'aulo *ghingras,*" p. 216, photo 1.
16. Wegner, *Musikleben,* Figs. 28a, 28b.
17. Ibid., pp. 66, 229; E. Keuls, "The Apulian Xylophone: A Mysterious Musical Instrument Identified," *American Journal of Archaeology* 83 (1979): 476–77.

Chapter V Music Theory

1. Andrew Barker, "*Hoi kaloumenoi harmonikoi:* The Predecessors of Aristoxenus," *Proceedings of the Cambridge Philological Society* 24 (1978): 1–21.
2. See Warren D. Anderson, "The Importance of Damonian Theory in Plato's Thought," *Transactions of the American Philological Association* 86 (1955): 88–102.
3. R. P. Winnington-Ingram, "The First Notational Diagram of Aristides Quintilianus," *Philologus* 117 (1973): 243–49. Also, M. Vogel, *Die Enharmonik der Griechen* (Dusseldorf, 1963).

4. Andrew Barker, "Music and Perception: A Study in Aristoxenus," *Journal of Hellenic Studies* 98 (1978): 9–15.

5. F. Zaminer, "Hypate, Mese, und Nete in frühgriechischen Denken: Ein altes musikterminologisches Problem in neuem Licht," *Archiv für Musikwissenschaft* 41 (1984): 1–26.

6. In general, see R. P. Winnington-Ingram, *Mode in Ancient Greek Music* (Oxford, 1936).

7. See L. E. Rossi, *Metrica e critica stilistica: Il termine "ciclico" e l'agoge ritmica* (Rome, 1963).

Chapter VI Texts with Musical Notation

1. A. Bataille, "Remarques sur les deux annotations mélodique de l'ancienne musique Grecque," *Recherche de Papyrologie* 1 (1961) 19.

2. S. Eitrem, L. Amundsen, and R. P. Winnington-Ingram, "Fragments of Unknown Greek Tragic Texts with Musical Notation (*POsl.* 1413)," *Symbolae Osloenses* 31 (1955): 77 ff., 85 ff.

3. O. M. Pearl and R. P. Winnington-Ingram, "A Michigan Papyrus with Musical Notation," *Journal of Egyptian Archaeology* 51 (1965): 192 ff.

4. Egert Pöhlmann, *Griechische Musikfragmente* (Nuremberg, 1960), 45.

5. Egert Pöhlmann, *Denkmäler altgriechischer Musik* (Nuremberg, 1970).

6. Published by Denise Jourdan-Hemmerdinger, "Un nouveau papyrus musical d'Euripide," *Comptes-Rendus des Séances de l'Académie des Inscriptions et des Belles Lettres* (Paris, 1973), 292–302.

7. See Giovanni Comotti, "Words, Verse, and Music in Euripides' *Iphigenia in Aulis*," *Museum Philologicum Londiniense* 2 (1977): 69–84, and Denise Jourdan-Hemmerdinger, "Le nouveau papyrus d'Euripide qu'apporte-t-il à la théorie et à l'histoire de la musique?" in *Les sources en musicologie* (Paris, 1981), 35–65. See also Thomas J. Mathiesen, "New Fragments of Ancient Greek Music," *Acta Musicologica* 53 (1981): 23–32.

8. See G. Marzi, "Il papiro musicale dell'*Oreste* di Euripide," in *Scritti in onore di L. Ronga* (Milan, 1973), 4–8.

9. See R. P. Winnington-Ingram, *Mode in Ancient Greek Music* (Oxford, 1936), 33–38.

10. Bruno Gentili, *Lo Spettacolo nel Mondo Antico*, 19 ff.

11. Bruno Gentili, "Rec. a POxy. 25 (1959)," *Gnomon* 33 (1961): 331–443.

12. M. W. Haslam, "Texts with Musical Notation," *Oxyrhynchus Papyri* 53 (London, 1986): 41–47.

13. Ibid., *Oxyrhynchus Papyri* 44 (London, 1976): 58–67.

14. Ibid., 67–72.

15. Ibid., *Oxyrhynchus Papyri* 53 (London, 1986): 47–48.

Sources

1. Cf. I. Düring, "Studies in Musical Terminology in Fifth-Century Literature," *Eranos* 43 (1945): 176–97.
2. See W. Crönert, "Die Hibehrede über die Musik," *Hermes* 44 (1909): 503–21.

Glossary

Words set in SMALL CAPS are defined elsewhere in the Glossary.

Anapaest. Foot consisting of two short syllables in the weak beat followed by one long syllable in the strong beat: ⏑⏑–.

Anapaestic rhythm. Rhythm of the even genre (see RHYTHMIC GENRE), with ascending progression (i.e., the weak beat precedes the strong beat: ⏑⏑–⏑⏑–, etc.).

Aulos. Wind instrument with one or two reeds, popular throughout the ancient world and most similar, among modern instruments, to the oboe.

Barbitos, baromos, barmos. Stringed instrument of the lyre family.

Chorde. The string of an instrument and the corresponding note. Each *chorde* had a distinct position and designation within the octave, which consisted of two disjunct TETRACHORDS.

Chromatic genus. Characterized by the arrangement of the intervals within the TETRACHORD according to the ascending succession of one semitone, one semitone, one and a half tones (chromatic *toniaion* or *syntonon*). In the soft chromatic (*malakon*), the first two intervals are reduced to ⅓ tone each, and in the chromatic hemiolion to ⅜ tone. See Aristox. *Harm.* 2.50–51, p. 63 Da Rios; *Anon. Bellermann* 53, p. 15, 9 ff. Najock.

161

Cretic. Foot consisting of a long and a short syllable in the strong beat, and of a long syllable in the weak beat (ratio 3:2, RHYTHMIC GENRE hemiolion): $-\smile-$.

Dactyl. Foot consisting of a long syllable in the strong beat followed by two short syllables in the weak beat: $-\smile\smile$.

Dactylic rhythm. Rhythm of the even genre (see RHYTHMIC GENRE) with descending progression (the strong beat precedes the weak beat: $-\smile\smile-\smile\smile$, etc.).

Diatonic genus. Characterized by the arrangement of the intervals within the TETRACHORD in the ascending succession of one semitone, one tone, one tone (diatonic *syntonon*). In the soft diatonic (*malakon*), the third note (*lichanos*) is moved so that the succession of the intervals is of 1 semitone, ¾ tone, ⅗ tone. See Aristox. *Harm.* 2.51, p. 64 Da Rios; *Anon. Bellermann* 54, pp. 59–61 Najock.

Double genre. See RHYTHMIC GENRE.

Elymoi. Type of AULOS.

Enharmonic genus. Characterized by the arrangement of the intervals within the TETRACHORD in the ascending succession of ¼ tone, ¼ tone, two tones. See Aristox. *Harm.* 2.50, p. 63 Da Rios.

Enoplian. Rhythm and *colon* with ascending progression (the weak beat precedes the strong beat), characterized by the freedom of the weak beats: $\smile\smile-\smile\smile-\smile\smile-\smile$.

Epitritic genre. See RHYTHMIC GENRE.

Even genre. See RHYTHMIC GENRE.

Harmonia. The original meaning of the term was "connection, joint." In the musical sense, it was first used to indicate the "tuning of an instrument" and consequently the "arrangement of the intervals in the octave." From the end of the sixth century B.C. (Lasus of Hermione) until the fourth century B.C. (Aristotle), *harmonia* (Aeolian, Dorian, Lydian, Phrygian, Ionian, etc.) referred to a combination of features that contributed to identifying the musical production of a certain geographical and cultural area. Plato (*Rep.* 3.398 ff.) and Aristotle (*Pol.* 8.1341b19 ff.) attributed to some of the harmoniae a specific moral value and an essential paideutic function. In Aristoxenus, *harmonia* is always used with the meaning "enharmonic genus." In the Pythagorean tradition, from Philolaus onward, the term designates the interval of an octave.

Hemiolion genre. See RHYTHMIC GENRE.

Hydraulis. Water organ, invented by Ctesibius of Alexandria in the third century B.C.

Iamb. Foot consisting of a short syllable in the weak beat followed by a long syllable in the strong beat: ˘ —.

Iambic rhythm. Rhythm of the double genre (see RHYTHMIC GENRE) with ascending progression (the weak beat precedes the strong beat: ˘ — ˘ —, etc.).

Kymbala. Percussion instrument.

Lyra. Stringed instrument, widespread throughout Greece from the earliest antiquity. See PHORMINX, BARBITOS (or BAROMOS or BARMOS).

Magadis. Instrument of the harp family, Asiatic in origin. *Magadis* was also the name of an AULOS with a broad sound range (Athen. 14.634b ff.).

Octave species (*eide tou dia pason*). See SYSTEM.

Paeon. Foot consisting of one long and three short syllables. First paeon: — ˘ ˘ ˘. Second paeon: ˘ — ˘ ˘. Third paeon: ˘ ˘ — ˘. Fourth paeon: ˘ ˘ ˘ —. It belongs to the hemiolion genre (see RHYTHMIC GENRE).

Pektis. Many-string instrument of the harp family akin to the MAGADIS and the SAMBYKE.

Phorminx. Stringed instrument of the LYRA family.

Prosodiac. Rhythm and *colon* with ascending progression (the weak beat precedes the strong beat) characterized by freedom of the weak beats. It represents the catalectic form of the ENOPLIAN: ≅ — ≅ — ≅ —. In ancient metrical and rhythmic terminology *enoplian* and *prosodiac* are often alternatively applied to the same sequences.

Rhombos. Instrument belonging to the category of aerophones. See *Etym. Mag.* s.v. *rhymbos*.

Rhythmic genre. Metrical and musical rhythm was produced by the succession of strong and weak beats ("descending" and "rising," respectively). The classification of rhythms according to genres can be traced back to Damon (mid-fifth century B.C.; cf. Plato *Rep.* 3.400b ff.). The unit of rhythmic measure is the foot, consisting in the association of two or more syllables (cf. Aristid. Quint. *De mus.* 1.14, p. 33, 12 Winnington-Ingram). The rhythmic genre is determined by the ratio within the foot between the duration of the strong beat and that of the weak beat, expressed in "times." The temporal unit is the primary time, *chronos protos,* which takes the time of a short syllable (˘). The long syllable (—) has double duration, while protracted syllables have triple (∪), quadruple (⊔), and quintuple (ɰ) duration with respect to the *chronos protos* (cf. *Anon. Bellermann* 1, p. 1 Najock). If the ratio is 1:1 the rhythm is of the even genre (lesser proceleusmatic ˘ ˘, dactyl — ˘ ˘, anapaest ˘ ˘ —, etc.). If the ratio is 2:1, the rhythm is of the double genre (iamb ⌣−, trochee −⌣, etc.). If the ratio is 3:2, the rhythm is of the hemiolion genre (cretic −⌣−, paeon −⌣⌣⌣, etc.). If the ratio is 4:3, the rhythm is of the epitritic genre (first epitrite ⌣−−−, second epitrite −⌣−−, etc.). Cf. Aristid. Quint. *De mus.* 1.14 ff., p. 32, 11 ff. Winnington-Ingram). Greek rhythmicologists regarded ratios different from the above as arhythmic, and tended to bring them back into the range of the four rhythmic genres by deconstructing and reconstructing their podal sequences. Cf. Aristid. Quint. *De mus.* 1.18, p. 38, 15 ff. Winnington-Ingram. Aristoxenus (*Rhythm.* p. 25, 14 ff. Pighi) also considered the epitritic genre as arhythmic.

Salpinx. Metal wind instrument of Etruscan origin. Cf. Athen. 4.184a ff.; Poll. *Onom.* 4.85.

Sambyke. Many-string instrument of the harp family, akin to the MAGADIS.

Synaulia. A term designating (1) the concert of two auletes that was held in Athens during the Panathenaea (Poll. *Onom.* 4.83); (2) the simultaneous playing of stringed instruments, especially the cithara, and of winds in the accompaniment of song or instrumental performance (Athen. 14.617f ff.). The first to introduce this type of instrumental association (also called *enaulos kitharisis*) were the disciples of Epigonus of Ambracia, a citharist of the sixth century B.C. (Athen. 14.637 f.).

System. Consecution of two or more intervals. The fundamental system of Greek music is the TETRACHORD. Larger systems are produced by the following associations: (a) two conjunct tetrachords; (b) two disjunct tetrachords (the octave); (c) three conjunct tetrachords plus a note (*proslambanomenos*) added below the lowest tetrachord—the lesser perfect system (*systema teleion elatton*); (d) four tetrachords conjunct two by two with a one-tone interval of disjunction in the middle, plus a note (*proslambanomenos*) added to the lowest tetrachord—the greater perfect system (*systema teleion meizon*). The lesser and greater perfect systems combined together in a single sequence of notes constitute the immutable perfect system (*systema teleion ametabolon*). Within the greater perfect system, it is possible to identify seven species of octave, which some scholars have arbitrarily identified with the traditional harmoniae.

Tetrachord. System of four consecutive notes comprised within an interval of a fourth (two and a half tones). The inner "movable" notes vary their position according to the genus (see CHROMATIC, DIATONIC, ENHARMONIC). Two consecutive tetrachords can be conjunct, when the fourth note of the first tetrachord coincides with the first note of the second; or disjunct, when the interval of a tone occurs between the two.

Tonos. In the language of musical theory, the term can mean (*a*) "tension of the string" and, therefore, "sound of a certain pitch, note" (Plat. *Rep.* 10.617b); (*b*) "interval of one tone" (Aristid. Quint. *De mus.* 17, p. 11, 1 Winnington-Ingram); or (*c*) "scale" (Aristox. *Harm.* 2.37, p. 46, 17 ff. Da Rios). In this last sense, *tonos* was used next to *tropos* to indicate the fifteen scales obtained by attributing the value of musical note to the CHORDAI of the immutable perfect system (see SYSTEM), and by transposing the resulting two-octave scale by a semitone at a time for all the semitones that are comprised in an octave plus a tone.

Trochaic rhythm. Rhythm of the double genre (see RHYTHMIC GENRE), with descending progression (the strong beat precedes the weak beat: ‒ ◡ ‒ ◡, etc.).

Trochee. Foot formed by the succession of a long syllable in a strong beat and a short one in a weak beat: ‒ ◡.

Tropos. See TONOS.

Tympanon. Percussion instrument.

Selected Bibliography

Bibliographical Surveys (arranged chronologically)

Fellerer, G. "Zur Erforschung der antiken Musik im 16.18 Jahrhundert." *Petersjahrbuch* 12 (1936): 84 ff.

Bucholz, H. *Bursians Jahresberichte* 5, 11 (1877): 1–33 [1873–77].

Velke, W. *Bursians Jahresberichte* 6, 15 (1878): 149–70 [1878].

Guhrauer, H. *Bursians Jahresberichte* 9, 28 (1881): 168–82 [1879–80].

———. *Bursians Jahresberichte* 13, 44 (1885): 1–35 [1881–84].

Von Jan, Carl. *Bursians Jahresberichte* 28, 104 (1900): 1–75 [1884–99].

Graf, E. *Bursians Jahresberichte* 31, 118 (1903): 212–35 [1899–1902].

Abert, H. *Bursians Jahresberichte* 37, 144 (1909): 1–74 [1903–8].

———. *Bursians Jahresberichte* 48, 193 (1922): 1–59 [1909–21].

Fellerer, G. *Bursians Jahresberichte* 61, 246 (1935): 1–42 [1921–31].

Winnington-Ingram, R. P. "Ancient Greek Music: A Bibliography, 1932–57." *Lustrum* 3 (1958): 5–57.

Mathiesen, Thomas J. *A Bibliography of Sources for the Study of Ancient Greek Music*. Music Indexes and Bibliographies. Volume 10. Hackensack, New Jersey, 1974.

Works of General Interest

Barker, Andrew, ed. *Greek Musical Writings*. Vol. 1, *The Musician and His Art*. Cambridge, 1984.

Chailley, J. *La musique grecque antique*. Paris, 1979.

Del Grande, C. *Espressione musicale dei poeti greci*. Naples, 1932.

———. "Grecia," *La Musica, Parte I: Enciclopedia Storica*. Turin, 1966. 2:603–25.

Gevaert, Fr. Aug. *Histoire et théorie de la musique de l'antiquité*. Vols. 1 and 2. Ghent, 1875–81; repr. Hildesheim, 1965.

Henderson, Isobel. "Ancient Greek Music." *New Oxford History of Music*. New York, 1957. 1:336–403.

Lippman, Edward. *Musical Thought in Ancient Greece*. New York, 1964.

Michaelides, Solon. *The Music of Ancient Greece: An Encyclopaedia*. London, 1978.

Mountford, J. E., and R. P. Winnington-Ingram. "Music." *Oxford Classical Dictionary*. 2d ed. Oxford, 1970. Pp. 705–13.

Neubecker, Annemarie Jeannette. *Altgriechische Musik: Eine Einführung*. Darmstadt, 1977.

Reinach, Théodor. *La musique grècque*. Paris, 1926.

Righini, P. *La musica greca: Analisi storico-tecnica*. Padua, 1976.

Ritoók, Zs. *Források az ókori görög zeneesztétika történetéhez*. Budapest, 1982.

Salazar, A. *La musica en la cultura griega*. Mexico City, 1954.

Sachs, Curt. *The History of Musical Instruments*. New York, 1940. Pp. 128–50.

———. *The Rise of Music in the Ancient World, East and West*. New York, 1943. Pp. 197–284.

Scott, J. E. "Roman Music." *The New Oxford History of Music*. Vol. 1. New York, 1957.

Tiby, O. *La musica in Grecia e a Roma*. Florence, 1942.

Vetter, W. *Antike Musik*. Munich, 1936.

———. "Griechenland: A. Antike Musik," *Die Musik in Geschichte und Gegenwart*. Kassel and Basel, 1956. 5:839–65.

Wille, G. *Musica Romana*. Amsterdam, 1967.

Winnington-Ingram, R. P. "Greek, Ancient." *The New Grove's Dictionary of Music and Musicians*. London, 1980. 7:659–72.

Editions of the Ancient Musical Theorists

Aristides Quintilianus. *De musica libri tres*. Ed. R. P. Winnington-Ingram. Leipzig, 1963.

Aristotle. *Problemi musicali*. Ed. G. Marenghi. Florence, 1957.

Aristoxenus. *Elementa harmonica*. Ed. R. da Rios. Rome, 1954.

———. *Rhythmica*. Ed. G. B. Pighi. Bologna, 1959.

Augustinus. *De musica libri sex.* Ed. G. Ginaert and F. J. Thonnard. Bruges, 1947.

Bellermann, F. *Anonyma de musica scripta Bellermanniana.* Ed. D. Najock. Leipzig, 1975.

Boethius. *De institutione musica libri quinque.* Ed. G. Friedlein. Leipzig, 1867.

Bryennius, M. *Harmonics.* Ed. G. H. Jonker. Groningen, 1970.

Cassiodorus. *Institutiones.* Ed. R. A. B. Mynors. Third Edition. Oxford, 1969.

Censorinus. *De die natali liber.* Ed. O. Jahn. Berlin, 1945. Repr. Hildesheim, 1963.

Martianus Capella. *De nuptiis Philologiae et Mercuri.* Ed. A. Dick and J. Préaux. Stuttgart, 1969.

Philodemus. *De musica librorum quae extant.* Ed. J. Kemke. Leipzig, 1884.

Porphyrius. *Kommentar zur Harmonielehre des Ptolemaios.* Ed. Ingemar Düring. Göteborg, 1930.

Ptolemy (Claudius Ptolemaeus). *Die Harmonielehre des Klaudios Ptolemaios.* Ed. Ingemar Düring. Göteborg, 1930.

Von Jan, Carl, ed., *Musici scriptores Greci.* Leipzig, 1895. [Contains the musical writings of Aristotle, Pseudo-Aristotle, Euclid, Cleionides, Nicomachus, Baccheius, Gaudentius, and Alypius.]

Index

ANCIENT SOCIETY AND HISTORY

The series Ancient Society and History offers books, relatively brief in compass, on selected topics in the history of ancient Greece and Rome, broadly conceived, with a special emphasis on comparative and other nontraditional approaches and methods. The series, which includes both works of synthesis and works of original scholarship, is aimed at the widest possible range of specialist and nonspecialist readers.

Published in the series:
Eva Cantarella, PANDORA'S DAUGHTERS: *The Role and Status of Women in Greek and Roman Antiquity*
Alan Watson, ROMAN SLAVE LAW
John E. Stambaugh, THE ANCIENT ROMAN CITY
Géza Alföldy, THE SOCIAL HISTORY OF ROME
Giovanni Comotti, MUSIC IN GREEK AND ROMAN CULTURE
Christian Habicht, CICERO THE POLITICIAN
Mark Golden, CHILDREN AND CHILDHOOD IN CLASSICAL ATHENS
Thomas Cole, THE ORIGINS OF RHETORIC IN ANCIENT GREECE
Maurizio Bettini, ANTHROPOLOGY AND ROMAN CULTURE: *Kinship, Time, Images of the Soul*